Bank Statement Mortgage Loans with Low Credit or Challenges

How to Get Approved Despite Credit Issues Using Alternative Documentation

By Joseph G. Correa

Licensed Mortgage Broker

Finibi Mortgage

Copyright & Legal Notice

Published by Live Stronger Faster

The information provided in this book is for educational and informational purposes only and does not constitute financial, legal, tax, or investment advice. Although the author is a licensed mortgage professional, the content presented is general in nature and is not intended as personalized guidance for any specific individual or financial situation.

The strategies, structuring methods, and examples discussed in this book are illustrative and educational in nature. They are intended to demonstrate concepts related to bank statement mortgage loan qualification and structuring, including deposit analysis, expense ratio application, and investor guideline interpretation. These examples do not represent guaranteed outcomes or approvals. Results may vary significantly based on individual financial profiles, documentation, credit history, property type, and lender-specific requirements.

The author and publisher make no representations or warranties regarding the accuracy, completeness, or applicability of the content and disclaim any liability for errors, omissions, or outcomes resulting from the use or misuse of the information contained in this book.

All trademarks, service marks, company names, and product names referenced in this publication are the property of their respective owners and are used strictly for identification and educational purposes only. Their inclusion does not imply endorsement or affiliation.

First Edition, 2026

Table of Contents

these timelines can be more flexible depending on the strength of the overall file. A borrower who experienced a bankruptcy or foreclosure but has since demonstrated consistent income, strong bank deposits, and financial stability may qualify sooner than expected. This shift in focus—from past mistakes to present performance—is one of the defining advantages of alternative documentation lending.

Beyond seasoning, compensating factors play a vital role in strengthening a mortgage application. These are elements within a borrower's profile that offset perceived risks and enhance overall eligibility. Examples include significant cash reserves, low debt-to-income ratios based on bank statement calculations, large down payments, stable business operations, or consistent deposit patterns over time. In many cases, a borrower with less-than-perfect credit can still achieve approval by presenting a well-structured file that highlights these strengths. This book will explore how to identify, develop, and leverage compensating factors to turn a challenging file into an approvable one.

Another key concept introduced in this book is the art of structuring stronger files. Mortgage approval is not simply about meeting minimum guidelines; it is about presenting a clear, logical, and compelling financial story. For borrowers with credit challenges, this becomes even more important.

Lenders and underwriters need to see not only that the borrower can afford the loan, but also that any past issues have been resolved and are unlikely to recur. This means carefully organizing bank statements, explaining anomalies, documenting improvements, and aligning all aspects of the file to support a consistent narrative of stability and growth.

One of the most empowering aspects of bank statement mortgage loans is their ability to provide second chances without sacrificing financial integrity. Unlike high-risk lending models that ignore underwriting discipline, non-QM bank statement programs still require thorough evaluation. The difference lies in how that evaluation is conducted. Instead of disqualifying borrowers based on rigid credit thresholds, lenders assess the full picture—income trends, business performance, liquidity, and overall financial behavior. This holistic approach creates a more accurate representation of a borrower's true risk and potential.

Throughout this book, you will discover that credit challenges do not have to define your financial future. They are, in many cases, temporary obstacles that can be overcome with the right strategy, documentation, and guidance. Whether you are a borrower seeking approval, a loan officer structuring deals, or an investor building a portfolio, understanding how to navigate credit issues within the bank statement loan framework is a powerful skill. It allows you to unlock opportunities that others may overlook and to create solutions where traditional systems see limitations.

It is also important to recognize the psychological aspect of credit challenges. Many borrowers carry a sense of discouragement or frustration after being denied by traditional lenders. They may believe that homeownership or refinancing is out of reach, not realizing that alternative solutions exist. This book aims to shift that mindset by providing clarity, confidence, and actionable strategies. When borrowers understand how the system works—and more importantly, how to work within it—they regain control of their financial path.

As you progress through this book, you will learn how to evaluate different types of credit issues and determine their impact on loan eligibility. You will explore strategies for improving a borrower's profile prior to application, including optimizing bank statement deposits, reducing visible risk factors, and strengthening compensating elements. You will also gain insight into how lenders interpret credit within the context of bank statement loans, allowing you to anticipate potential concerns and address them proactively.

Additionally, this book will guide you through real-world scenarios that demonstrate how borrowers with credit challenges can successfully secure financing. These examples will illustrate not only the technical aspects of structuring loans, but also the strategic thinking required to present a strong application. By analyzing these scenarios, you will develop the ability to approach complex cases with confidence and creativity, transforming obstacles into opportunities.

The goal of this introduction—and the book as a whole—is to redefine what is possible. Bank statement mortgage loans are not simply an alternative; they are a powerful tool for expanding access to financing in a way that reflects the realities of modern income and financial behavior. For borrowers with credit challenges, they represent a path forward—one that values resilience, growth, and current performance over past imperfections.

In the chapters ahead, you will gain a comprehensive understanding of how to navigate credit issues, leverage compensating factors, and structure loan files that stand up to underwriting scrutiny. You will learn how to think like an underwriter, anticipate lender expectations, and position each application for success. Most importantly, you will discover that approval is not about perfection—it is about preparation, presentation, and persistence. This is your opportunity to master one of the most valuable areas within the bank statement mortgage loan space. Whether you are rebuilding your own financial profile or helping others achieve their goals, the knowledge contained in this book will equip you with the tools to succeed. Credit challenges may be part of the journey, but they do not have to be the destination. With the right approach, they can become stepping stones toward financial growth, real estate ownership, and long-term wealth creation.

Chapter 1

Understanding Credit Challenges in Bank Statement Mortgage Loans

The foundation of successfully navigating bank statement mortgage loans for borrowers with credit challenges begins with a clear and realistic understanding of how credit is viewed in the lending world. Credit is not simply a number; it is a behavioral record that reflects patterns, decisions, timing, and sometimes unexpected life events. In traditional mortgage lending, credit scores often act as gatekeepers, determining eligibility before the full financial story is even considered. However, in the world of bank statement mortgage loans, credit is repositioned. It still matters, but it is no longer the sole authority. Instead, it becomes one of several factors evaluated within a broader, more flexible underwriting framework.

To understand this shift, it is important to first break down what constitutes a credit challenge. Credit challenges can include late payments, collections, charge-offs, high credit card utilization, limited credit history, bankruptcies, foreclosures, short sales, or even inconsistent credit usage patterns. Each of these items tells a story, but not all stories carry the same weight. For example, a single late payment two years ago is vastly different from multiple recent delinquencies. A borrower who experienced a foreclosure during a major economic downturn but has since rebuilt their income and savings profile is also very different from a borrower currently struggling to manage ongoing obligations. The key in bank statement lending is context.

Context allows lenders to evaluate whether a borrower's past credit issues are isolated events or ongoing risks. This is where the concept of trend analysis becomes essential. Instead of focusing solely on what happened, lenders examine what has happened since. Has the borrower demonstrated consistent deposits? Have they stabilized their business income? Have they maintained current accounts in good standing? These forward-looking indicators often carry more weight than older credit events, especially when supported by strong bank statement documentation.

One of the most important distinctions in this space is the difference between "recoverable" credit issues and "active" credit risk. Recoverable issues are those that occurred in the past and have since been resolved or stabilized. Examples include a bankruptcy that has been discharged, a foreclosure that occurred several years ago, or a period of high utilization that has since been reduced. Active credit risk, on the other hand, includes ongoing delinquencies, frequent missed payments, or escalating debt obligations. Bank statement mortgage lenders are far more willing to work with recoverable issues than active risks, especially when the borrower can demonstrate strong current cash flow.

Another critical concept is credit event seasoning. Seasoning refers to the amount of time that has passed since a negative credit event occurred. In traditional lending, seasoning requirements are often rigid, with strict timelines that must be met before a borrower becomes eligible again. In contrast, bank statement mortgage loans often provide more flexibility, allowing borrowers to qualify sooner if they can demonstrate compensating strengths. For example, a borrower who experienced a bankruptcy two years ago but now shows consistent monthly deposits, strong reserves, and stable business income may be considered a viable candidate under certain non-QM programs.

It is also important to understand that not all credit scores are treated equally. A borrower with a 620 credit score supported by strong bank statements, significant reserves, and a low calculated debt-to-income ratio may present a stronger overall profile than a borrower with a higher credit score but unstable income. This is one of the key advantages of bank statement lending—it prioritizes the borrower's ability to repay based on real cash flow rather than relying solely on a numerical score.

Debt-to-income ratio, or DTI, is another area where bank statement loans differ significantly. Instead of using tax returns to calculate income, lenders analyze deposits from bank statements and apply an expense factor to determine usable income. This method often results in a more accurate representation of a borrower's true earning capacity, particularly for self-employed individuals who may write off expenses on their tax returns. When combined with manageable debt obligations, this can significantly strengthen a borrower's profile, even in the presence of credit challenges.

Compensating factors play a major role in offsetting credit concerns. These factors act as strengths within the file that reduce perceived risk and increase the likelihood of approval. Examples include large down payments, substantial cash reserves, long-term business stability, consistent deposit patterns, and low leverage. For borrowers with credit challenges, compensating factors can often be the deciding factor between approval and denial. A well-structured file that highlights these strengths can effectively shift the focus away from past credit issues and toward current financial capability.

The structure of the loan itself also plays a role in managing risk. Borrowers with credit challenges may be required to provide larger down payments or maintain higher reserve requirements. These measures not only protect the lender but also demonstrate the borrower's financial discipline and commitment. In many cases, borrowers who are willing to meet these conditions gain access to opportunities that would otherwise be unavailable through traditional lending channels.

Another important aspect of understanding credit challenges is recognizing the impact of documentation and presentation. A borrower's financial profile is only as strong as the way it is presented to the underwriter. Clear, organized bank statements, consistent deposit patterns, and well-documented explanations for any anomalies can significantly improve the outcome of a loan application. For borrowers with credit challenges, this level of preparation becomes even more critical. Every detail matters, and every inconsistency must be addressed proactively.

This chapter also emphasizes the importance of mindset. Borrowers with credit challenges often approach the mortgage process with hesitation or uncertainty, assuming that past issues will automatically disqualify them. However, the reality is that bank statement mortgage loans are designed to provide alternative pathways to approval. By understanding how these loans work and how credit is evaluated within this framework, borrowers can approach the process with confidence and clarity. Ultimately, the goal of this chapter is to establish a strong foundation for the rest of the book. Credit challenges are not barriers; they are variables that must be understood, managed, and strategically addressed. With the right knowledge, preparation, and approach, borrowers can transform perceived weaknesses into opportunities for approval. The chapters that follow will build upon this foundation, providing actionable strategies for structuring stronger files, leveraging compensating factors, and navigating the underwriting process with confidence.

Real-Life Math Example: Structuring a Loan with Credit Challenges Using Bank Statement Income

Let's consider a real-world scenario involving a self-employed borrower named Carlos, who owns a small construction business. Carlos has been in business for over five years and generates strong monthly revenue, but his credit profile reflects challenges from the past. Three years ago, Carlos experienced a temporary downturn in his business, which resulted in several late payments and high credit card utilization. His current credit score is 635. While this score would limit his options in traditional lending, Carlos is a strong candidate for a bank statement mortgage loan due to his consistent income and improving financial profile.

Carlos is looking to purchase a primary residence valued at $500,000. He is prepared to put down 20%, which equals $100,000. This leaves a loan amount of $400,000. His lender requires 12 months of business bank statements to calculate his income. Over the past 12 months, Carlos has deposited a total of $240,000 into his business account. This averages to $20,000 per month in gross deposits.

The lender applies an expense factor of 50% to account for business expenses. This means that 50% of Carlos's deposits are considered usable income. Based on this calculation, his qualifying monthly income is $10,000. This figure is used to determine his debt-to-income ratio.

Carlos has existing monthly debts totaling $2,000, including car payments, credit cards, and a small business loan. The estimated monthly mortgage payment for his new home, including principal, interest, taxes, and insurance, is $3,000. When combined, his total monthly obligations equal $5,000.

To calculate his debt-to-income ratio, we divide his total monthly obligations by his qualifying income. In this case, $5,000 divided by $10,000 results in a 50% DTI. While this is higher than traditional lending guidelines, it is acceptable within many bank statement loan programs, especially when supported by strong compensating factors.

Carlos also has $50,000 in reserves after his down payment and closing costs. These reserves represent approximately 10 months of mortgage payments, which significantly strengthens his profile. Additionally, his business has shown consistent deposit patterns over the past year, with no significant declines or irregularities.

Despite his credit challenges, Carlos's overall financial profile tells a compelling story. His income is stable, his business is performing well, and he has demonstrated the ability to manage his finances effectively over time. The combination of strong bank statement income, sufficient reserves, and a solid down payment offsets the risk associated with his credit score.

From an underwriting perspective, Carlos's file is structured to highlight strengths while addressing weaknesses. His past credit issues are seasoned, his current accounts are in good standing, and his financial trajectory is positive. The lender views him as a borrower who has recovered and stabilized, rather than one who presents ongoing risk.

As a result, Carlos is approved for the loan with slightly adjusted terms, including a modestly higher interest rate to account for his credit profile. However, this rate is still competitive within the non-QM space and allows him to achieve his goal of homeownership.

This example demonstrates how bank statement mortgage loans create opportunities for borrowers with credit challenges. By focusing on real income, applying strategic calculations, and leveraging compensating factors, borrowers like Carlos can successfully navigate the mortgage process and secure financing that aligns with their current financial reality.

Chapter 2

Credit Event Seasoning and Timeline Strategies for Approval

One of the most important concepts in successfully qualifying for a bank statement mortgage loan with credit challenges is understanding credit event seasoning. Seasoning refers to the amount of time that has passed since a negative credit event occurred, and it plays a critical role in how lenders evaluate risk. While traditional mortgage programs often rely on strict and inflexible timelines, the bank statement loan space introduces a more dynamic and strategic approach. In this world, time is not just a requirement–it is a tool that, when used correctly, can transform a previously ineligible borrower into a strong candidate for approval.

To fully grasp the importance of seasoning, it is necessary to understand how lenders interpret risk over time. When a negative credit event occurs–such as a bankruptcy, foreclosure, short sale, or series of late payments–it signals a period of financial instability. However, as time passes and the borrower demonstrates improved financial behavior, that initial signal begins to lose its weight. The longer the borrower maintains stability after the event, the more confidence lenders gain in their ability to repay a new mortgage. This gradual shift in perception is what makes seasoning such a powerful factor in bank statement lending.

Unlike traditional loans that may require fixed waiting periods of four to seven years after major credit events, many bank statement mortgage programs offer more flexible timelines. For example, a borrower who experienced a bankruptcy may be eligible for financing in as little as one to two years, provided they can demonstrate strong compensating factors. These factors may include consistent bank deposits, stable or increasing income, low current debt obligations, and significant reserves. The key is not just the passage of time, but what the borrower has done with that time.

Seasoning is not limited to major credit events. It also applies to patterns within a borrower's credit profile. For instance, a borrower who had multiple late payments within the past year may still qualify if those late payments are isolated to a specific period and are followed by a consistent record of on-time payments. In this case, the seasoning period begins from the last negative event. The lender evaluates how much time has passed since that point and whether the borrower has demonstrated a meaningful improvement in financial behavior.

This introduces an important strategy: controlling the

timeline. Borrowers and loan professionals who understand seasoning can strategically time a mortgage application to maximize approval chances. For example, waiting an additional three to six months after the last late payment can significantly improve the overall profile. During that time, the borrower can focus on strengthening other aspects of the file, such as increasing reserves, reducing debt, and maintaining consistent deposit patterns. This proactive approach turns time into an asset rather than a limitation.

Another critical aspect of seasoning is the concept of "event isolation." Lenders prefer to see that a negative credit event was caused by a specific, identifiable circumstance rather than an ongoing pattern of poor financial management. For example, a borrower who experienced financial hardship due to a temporary business disruption, medical emergency, or economic downturn may be viewed more favorably if they can demonstrate recovery and stability afterward. Documenting this narrative through clear explanations and supporting evidence can significantly enhance the borrower's credibility.

Bank statement mortgage lenders also pay close attention to how a borrower's financial profile evolves after a credit event. This includes analyzing bank statement deposits, business performance, and liquidity. A borrower who shows increasing deposits over time, consistent revenue streams, and disciplined financial behavior sends a strong signal that they have moved beyond their previous challenges. This forward-looking analysis is a defining characteristic of non-QM lending and one of the reasons why seasoning can be more flexible in this space.

It is also important to understand that not all seasoning is measured equally. Different types of credit events carry different levels of severity and therefore require different levels of recovery. For example, a single late payment may require only a short seasoning period, while a foreclosure may require a longer timeline to demonstrate stability. However, even in cases of more severe events, strong compensating factors can shorten the effective seasoning period. A borrower with a recent foreclosure but significant reserves, a large down payment, and strong bank statement income may still qualify under certain programs.

Another layer to consider is the interaction between seasoning and loan structure. Borrowers with shorter seasoning periods may face stricter terms, such as higher down payment requirements, higher interest rates, or additional reserve requirements. These adjustments allow lenders to manage risk while still providing access to financing. For borrowers, understanding this trade-off is essential. It allows them to make informed decisions about whether to proceed immediately or wait longer to secure more favorable terms. Seasoning also plays a role in investor guidelines. Different lenders and investors have varying levels of tolerance for credit events and their associated timelines. Some programs are designed specifically for borrowers with recent credit challenges, while others require longer seasoning periods. This creates an opportunity for strategic lender selection. By matching the borrower's profile with the right program, it is possible to achieve approval even in complex scenarios.

Documentation is another critical component of seasoning. Lenders often require detailed explanations for past credit events, along with supporting documentation that demonstrates resolution and recovery. This may include discharge papers for bankruptcies, settlement statements for foreclosures or short sales, and written explanations outlining the circumstances and subsequent improvements. A well-prepared explanation can transform a perceived weakness into a story of resilience and growth.

In addition to documenting past events, borrowers must also demonstrate current stability. This includes maintaining consistent bank statement deposits, avoiding new credit issues, and managing existing obligations responsibly. Even a small setback during the seasoning period—such as a new late payment—can reset the timeline and negatively impact the application. This highlights the importance of discipline and consistency during the recovery phase. From a strategic perspective, seasoning should be viewed as part of a broader approval plan. Borrowers should not simply wait for time to pass; they should actively use that time to strengthen their profile. This may involve optimizing business deposits, reducing unnecessary expenses, building reserves, and improving overall financial organization. By the time the application is submitted, the borrower should present a profile that clearly demonstrates stability, growth, and readiness for approval.

Ultimately, credit event seasoning is about transformation. It represents the journey from financial instability to stability, from risk to reliability, and from rejection to approval. In the bank statement mortgage loan space, this journey is not defined by rigid timelines but by measurable progress. Borrowers who understand and leverage seasoning can position themselves for success, even in the face of past challenges.

As you move forward, it is essential to remember that time alone is not enough. It is what you do with that time that matters. By combining strategic timing with strong financial behavior and thoughtful documentation, you can turn seasoning into one of your greatest advantages. The next sections of this book will build on this foundation, showing you how to align seasoning with compensating factors and file structuring to achieve consistent approvals.

Real-Life Math Example: Timing a Loan Approval After a Credit Event

Let's walk through a detailed real-life scenario involving a borrower named Sophia, a self-employed marketing consultant. Sophia experienced a significant financial setback two years ago when several of her largest clients paused contracts during an economic slowdown. As a result, she fell behind on her credit card payments and ultimately settled several accounts. Her credit score dropped to 610 at its lowest point.

Over the past two years, Sophia has rebuilt her business and now generates strong and consistent income. She is looking to purchase a home valued at $600,000 and plans to use a bank statement mortgage loan. She has saved $120,000 for a down payment, which represents 20% of the purchase price. This leaves a loan amount of $480,000.

Sophia's lender requires 12 months of personal bank statements. Over the past year, she has deposited a total of $300,000 into her account, averaging $25,000 per month.

The lender applies an expense factor of 40%, resulting in a qualifying monthly income of $15,000.

Her monthly debts total $3,000, including car payments and remaining credit obligations. The estimated mortgage payment for her new home is $3,500. This brings her total monthly obligations to $6,500. Dividing this by her qualifying income of $15,000 results in a debt-to-income ratio of approximately 43%.

At first glance, Sophia appears to be a strong candidate. However, her credit history still reflects the settlements from two years ago. The lender's guidelines require at least 24 months of seasoning for settled accounts, but they also consider compensating factors for borrowers who are slightly below this threshold.

At the time of her initial application, Sophia is 22 months removed from her last settlement. She is just two months short of the preferred seasoning period. The lender evaluates her file and identifies strong compensating factors, including her high income, consistent deposits, and significant down payment. However, they also note that waiting an additional two months would place her firmly within the preferred guidelines and potentially improve her loan terms.

Sophia decides to delay her application by two months. During this time, she continues to maintain consistent deposits, avoids new debt, and increases her reserves by saving an additional $10,000. By the time she reapplies, she is 24 months removed from her last credit event. This small adjustment in timing has a measurable impact. With the additional seasoning, the lender views her file as lower risk. As a result, she qualifies for a slightly lower interest rate, which reduces her monthly mortgage payment from $3,500 to $3,300. Over the life of the loan, this difference translates into tens of thousands of dollars in savings.

Let's quantify this impact. The $200 monthly savings results in $2,400 per year. Over a 30-year loan term, this equals $72,000 in total savings. This demonstrates how strategic timing and understanding seasoning can have a significant financial benefit.

Additionally, Sophia's improved profile allows her to maintain more favorable reserve requirements, giving her greater financial flexibility after closing. Her total reserves now cover approximately 12 months of mortgage payments, further strengthening her position.

This example illustrates the power of timing in the loan approval process. By understanding credit event seasoning and making a small strategic adjustment, Sophia was able to improve both her approval outcome and her long-term financial position. It also highlights the importance of combining mathematical analysis with strategic decision-making, ensuring that every aspect of the loan process is optimized for success.

Chapter 3

Compensating Factors That Turn Declines Into Approvals

In the world of bank statement mortgage loans, especially for borrowers with credit challenges, approval is rarely determined by a single factor. Instead, it is the combination of strengths within a file that creates a compelling case for approval. These strengths are known as compensating factors, and they are one of the most powerful tools available to borrowers and loan professionals. While credit issues may raise concerns, compensating factors provide the balance needed to offset those concerns and demonstrate that the borrower is still a strong candidate for financing.

Compensating factors are essentially positive elements within a borrower's financial profile that reduce perceived risk. They help lenders feel confident that, despite certain weaknesses—such as lower credit scores or past credit events—the borrower has the ability and stability to repay the loan. In bank statement lending, where flexibility is built into the underwriting process, these factors carry significant weight and can often be the deciding element between approval and denial. One of the most impactful compensating factors is strong and consistent bank statement income. Since bank statement loans rely on deposits rather than tax returns, the pattern and stability of those deposits become critical. A borrower who shows steady or increasing deposits over a 12- or 24-month period demonstrates reliability and business stability. Even if their credit score is below traditional thresholds, this consistency signals to the lender that the borrower has a dependable income stream that supports repayment.

Closely tied to income is the concept of cash reserves. Reserves refer to the amount of liquid assets a borrower has remaining after closing, typically measured in months of mortgage payments. For example, if a borrower's monthly housing payment is $4,000 and they have $40,000 in reserves, they effectively have 10 months of reserves. This is a powerful indicator of financial security. Borrowers with credit challenges who can demonstrate significant reserves are often viewed more favorably because they have a financial cushion to absorb unexpected expenses or temporary income disruptions.

Another key compensating factor is the size of the down payment. A larger down payment reduces the lender's risk by lowering the loan-to-value ratio. For instance, a borrower who puts down 25% or 30% instead of the minimum required amount significantly decreases the likelihood of default from the lender's perspective. This is especially important for borrowers with credit challenges, as it shows both financial discipline and a strong commitment to the property.

Debt management is also a critical component. Even if a borrower has a history of credit issues, their current debt profile can tell a different story. A borrower with low or manageable monthly obligations relative to their income presents less risk. In bank statement lending, where income is calculated based on deposits, maintaining a reasonable debt-to-income ratio is essential. Borrowers who proactively reduce debt prior to applying can dramatically improve their chances of approval.

Business stability is another often overlooked but highly influential factor. For self-employed borrowers, lenders look for consistency in business operations. This includes the length of time the business has been active, the stability of income, and the overall trajectory of deposits. A borrower who has been operating the same business for several years with consistent or growing revenue demonstrates reliability, even if their credit profile has imperfections.

Liquidity beyond reserves can also strengthen a file. This includes additional assets such as investment accounts, retirement funds, or other accessible capital. While not always required, these assets provide an extra layer of security and reassurance to the lender. They indicate that the borrower has multiple financial resources available, reducing the overall risk of default.

Another powerful compensating factor is the borrower's payment history on housing. A borrower who has consistently made rent or mortgage payments on time, even if they have had issues with other types of credit, demonstrates a priority for housing obligations. This behavioral pattern can be very persuasive in underwriting, as it suggests that the borrower is likely to continue prioritizing their mortgage payments in the future.

Documentation and organization also play a significant role. A well-prepared file that clearly presents income, explains anomalies, and provides supporting documentation can make a substantial difference. Underwriters are more likely to approve a loan when the file is easy to understand and tells a consistent, logical story. For borrowers with credit challenges, this level of clarity is essential.

It is also important to recognize that compensating factors are not evaluated in isolation. They work together to create an overall risk profile. For example, a borrower with a lower credit score may still be approved if they have strong income, significant reserves, and a large down payment. Conversely, a borrower with only one strong factor may not be sufficient to offset multiple weaknesses. The goal is to build a balanced and compelling file that addresses potential concerns from multiple angles.

Strategic planning is key when leveraging compensating factors. Borrowers should not simply rely on what they currently have; they should actively work to strengthen their profile before applying. This may involve saving additional funds to increase reserves, paying down debt to improve DTI, or ensuring that bank statement deposits are consistent and well-documented. Even small improvements can have a meaningful impact on the overall strength of the file.

Another important aspect is understanding how different lenders weigh compensating factors. Not all programs are the same, and some lenders may place greater emphasis on certain elements than others. This creates an opportunity to match the borrower's strengths with the right program. By aligning the file with a lender that values the borrower's specific compensating factors, the chances of approval can be significantly increased.

Ultimately, compensating factors represent the bridge between imperfection and approval. They allow borrowers to move beyond the limitations of their credit profile and demonstrate their true financial capability. In the bank statement mortgage loan space, where flexibility and creativity are essential, these factors become the foundation of successful loan structuring. As you continue through this book, it is important to remember that no file is perfect. Every borrower has strengths and weaknesses. The key is to identify those strengths, enhance them where possible, and present them in a way that tells a clear and compelling story. When done correctly, compensating factors can transform a challenging file into a strong approval, opening the door to homeownership, investment opportunities, and long-term financial growth.

Real-Life Math Example: Using Compensating Factors to Offset Credit Challenges

Let's examine a detailed real-world scenario involving a borrower named Daniel, a self-employed landscaper with a growing business. Daniel has been in business for four years and generates strong seasonal income. However, his credit score is 625 due to high credit card utilization and several late payments from two years ago. Despite these challenges, Daniel is determined to purchase an investment property valued at $450,000.

Daniel plans to put down 25%, which equals $112,500. This leaves a loan amount of $337,500. His lender requires 12 months of business bank statements. Over the past year, Daniel has deposited $180,000 into his account, averaging $15,000 per month. The lender applies an expense factor of 50%, resulting in a qualifying monthly income of $7,500. Daniel's current monthly debts total $1,500, including vehicle payments and remaining credit obligations. The estimated monthly mortgage payment for the investment property is $2,800. This brings his total monthly obligations to $4,300.

To calculate his debt-to-income ratio, we divide $4,300 by $7,500, resulting in approximately 57%. While this is on the higher end, it is still within acceptable limits for certain bank statement loan programs, particularly when supported by strong compensating factors.

Now let's evaluate Daniel's compensating factors. First, his down payment of 25% significantly reduces the lender's risk by lowering the loan-to-value ratio. Second, Daniel has $60,000 in reserves after closing, which equates to over 21 months of mortgage payments. This is a substantial financial cushion that provides strong reassurance to the lender.

Additionally, Daniel's business has shown consistent growth, with deposits increasing from $12,000 per month at the beginning of the year to $18,000 per month in recent months.

This upward trend indicates a positive trajectory and strengthens his income profile.

Daniel also takes a strategic step to improve his file before applying. He pays down $10,000 in credit card debt, reducing his monthly obligations by $300. This lowers his total monthly debt from $4,300 to $4,000. Recalculating his DTI, we divide $4,000 by $7,500, resulting in approximately 53%.

This seemingly small adjustment has a meaningful impact. A lower DTI improves his risk profile and increases the likelihood of approval. Additionally, reducing his credit card balances improves his credit score slightly, further strengthening his application.

Let's quantify the impact of his compensating factors. Without his large down payment and reserves, Daniel's file would likely be considered too risky due to his credit score and higher DTI. However, with a 25% down payment, over 20 months of reserves, and improving income trends, the lender views him as a strong candidate despite his credit challenges.

Daniel is approved for the loan, though with a slightly higher interest rate due to his credit profile. The rate results in a monthly payment of $2,800. If his credit were higher, he might have qualified for a payment of $2,600. The $200 difference equates to $2,400 per year.

However, Daniel plans to refinance in the future once his credit improves. By maintaining consistent payments and reducing his overall debt, he expects to qualify for a lower rate within two to three years. This strategy allows him to move forward with his investment now while positioning himself for better terms later.

Over a three-year period, the additional cost of the higher rate totals $7,200. However, the property generates $3,500 per month in rental income, resulting in a positive cash flow of $700 per month after expenses. Over three years, this equals $25,200 in net income.

When we compare the additional interest cost of $7,200 to the rental income of $25,200, Daniel still comes out ahead by $18,000. This demonstrates how strategic use of compensating factors can not only secure approval but also create profitable opportunities.

This example highlights the power of combining multiple strengths within a file. By leveraging a large down payment, strong reserves, improving income trends, and proactive debt reduction, Daniel was able to overcome his credit challenges and achieve his investment goals. It reinforces the idea that approval is not about perfection—it is about building a balanced and compelling financial profile that demonstrates the ability to succeed.

Chapter 4

Structuring Stronger Files for Underwriting Approval

In the world of bank statement mortgage loans, especially when working with borrowers who have credit challenges, structuring the loan file correctly is often more important than the raw numbers themselves. A borrower may have strong income, acceptable credit, and sufficient assets, but if the file is poorly structured or inconsistently presented, it can lead to unnecessary delays, conditions, or even a denial. On the other hand, a borrower with multiple challenges can still achieve approval if the file is organized, logical, and strategically built to highlight strengths while minimizing perceived risk. Structuring a stronger file is both an art and a science, and mastering it is one of the most valuable skills in alternative mortgage lending.

At its core, file structuring is about storytelling. Every mortgage file tells a story about the borrower's financial life. The underwriter's job is to evaluate whether that story supports the borrower's ability to repay the loan. If the story is unclear, inconsistent, or filled with gaps, the underwriter will naturally become more cautious. However, if the story is clear, well-documented, and supported by consistent data, the underwriter is far more likely to move toward approval. This is especially critical when the borrower has credit challenges, as the file must overcome initial skepticism by presenting a compelling and coherent narrative.

The first step in structuring a strong file is ensuring consistency across all documentation. Bank statement deposits, business activity, credit reports, and asset statements should all align with each other. For example, if a borrower claims to earn $20,000 per month based on bank statements, the deposits should reflect that level of activity consistently. Any large fluctuations, unexplained gaps, or irregular deposits can raise questions. These questions do not automatically lead to denial, but they must be addressed proactively with clear explanations and supporting documentation.

Deposit analysis is a central component of bank statement loan structuring. Lenders typically review 12 or 24 months of bank statements to determine income. However, not all deposits are treated equally. Transfers between accounts, one-time deposits, or irregular large sums may be excluded from income calculations unless properly documented. A well-structured file identifies and categorizes deposits clearly, ensuring that only eligible income is used while providing explanations for any anomalies. This level of detail reduces confusion and builds confidence in the borrower's income profile. Another critical aspect of structuring is the application of the expense factor. Since bank statement loans do not rely on tax returns, lenders apply an expense ratio to determine net income. This ratio can vary depending on the type of business, documentation provided, and lender guidelines. A borrower who can justify a lower expense ratio—through a CPA-prepared profit and loss statement, for example—can significantly increase their qualifying income. Structuring the file to support a favorable expense factor is a key strategy in maximizing approval potential.

Credit explanations also play a major role in file structuring. For borrowers with credit challenges, it is essential to provide clear, concise, and credible explanations for past issues. These explanations should not be overly detailed or emotional, but rather factual and focused on resolution. For example, a borrower who experienced late payments due to a temporary business downturn should explain the cause, the steps taken to resolve it, and the evidence of improved financial stability since then. When paired with strong bank statements and compensating factors, these explanations help shift the focus from past problems to current performance.

Asset positioning is another powerful tool in structuring a strong file. Assets are not just about meeting minimum requirements; they are about demonstrating financial strength and stability. Organizing assets in a way that highlights liquidity, reserves, and accessibility can significantly improve the borrower's profile. For example, showing multiple months of reserves in easily accessible accounts provides reassurance to the lender that the borrower can handle unexpected expenses or income fluctuations.

The structure of the loan itself must also be carefully considered. Adjusting elements such as the down payment, loan amount, or property type can have a significant impact on approval. For instance, increasing the down payment reduces the loan-to-value ratio and lowers risk. Choosing a property with strong income potential or stable value can also strengthen the overall file. These adjustments are not just financial decisions; they are strategic moves that align the loan with lender preferences and guidelines.

Another key element is the management of liabilities. Reducing or restructuring debt prior to applying can improve the debt-to-income ratio and strengthen the file. This may involve paying down credit cards, consolidating loans, or eliminating unnecessary obligations. Even small reductions in monthly debt can have a meaningful impact on the overall profile, making the file more attractive to lenders. Timing is also a critical factor in file structuring. Submitting a loan application at the right moment—when bank statements are strong, credit is stable, and assets are well-positioned—can significantly improve the chances of approval. Conversely, applying too early, before certain issues are resolved or optimized, can lead to avoidable challenges. Strategic timing allows the borrower to present the strongest possible version of their financial profile.

Documentation clarity cannot be overstated. Every document in the file should be organized, labeled, and easy to interpret. Underwriters often review multiple files simultaneously, and a well-organized file stands out immediately. Clear documentation reduces the need for additional conditions and speeds up the approval process. For borrowers with credit challenges, this clarity is especially important, as it helps build trust and confidence in the file.

Communication between the borrower, loan officer, and lender is another essential component of strong file structuring. Anticipating potential questions and addressing them upfront can prevent delays and misunderstandings. This includes providing explanations, additional documentation, and context where needed. A proactive approach ensures that the file moves smoothly through underwriting rather than getting stalled by avoidable issues.

Ultimately, structuring a stronger file is about control. While borrowers may not be able to change their past credit history, they can control how their current financial situation is presented. By focusing on consistency, clarity, and strategic alignment with lender guidelines, it is possible to transform a challenging file into a compelling case for approval.

This chapter reinforces the idea that approval is not just about meeting requirements—it is about exceeding expectations. A well-structured file does more than satisfy guidelines; it tells a story of stability, growth, and reliability. As you continue through this book, you will build on these principles, learning how to refine and optimize every aspect of the loan process to achieve consistent and successful outcomes.

Real-Life Math Example: Structuring a File for Approval with Strategic Adjustments

Let's examine a detailed real-world scenario involving a borrower named Olivia, a self-employed graphic designer. Olivia has been in business for three years and generates strong income, but her credit score is 630 due to past late payments and high credit card utilization. She is looking to purchase a primary residence valued at $550,000.

Initially, Olivia plans to put down 15%, which equals $82,500. This results in a loan amount of $467,500. Her lender requires 12 months of personal bank statements. Over the past year,

Olivia has deposited $264,000 into her account, averaging $22,000 per month.

The lender applies a standard expense factor of 50%, resulting in a qualifying monthly income of $11,000. Olivia's current monthly debts total $3,200, including credit cards, a car loan, and student loans. The estimated monthly mortgage payment for her new home is $3,400, bringing her total monthly obligations to $6,600.

To calculate her debt-to-income ratio, we divide $6,600 by $11,000, resulting in a DTI of 60%. This is higher than most lender guidelines and presents a challenge for approval.

Now, let's explore how structuring adjustments can improve Olivia's file. First, she works with her loan officer to identify opportunities to reduce her DTI. She pays off $8,000 in credit card debt, which lowers her monthly obligations by $400. This reduces her total monthly debt from $6,600 to $6,200.

Next, Olivia obtains a CPA-prepared profit and loss statement that supports a lower expense ratio of 40% instead of 50%. This increases her qualifying income from $11,000 to $13,200 per month.

Recalculating her DTI with these adjustments, we divide $6,200 by $13,200, resulting in approximately 47%. This is a significant improvement and falls within acceptable guidelines for many bank statement loan programs.

Olivia also decides to increase her down payment from 15% to 20%, contributing an additional $27,500. This reduces her loan amount to $440,000 and lowers her monthly mortgage payment from $3,400 to $3,100.

With the new mortgage payment, her total monthly obligations decrease to $5,900. Dividing $5,900 by her updated income of $13,200 results in a DTI of approximately 45%.

Let's summarize the impact of these adjustments. Initially, Olivia's DTI was 60%, making approval unlikely. After strategic structuring, her DTI is reduced to 45%, significantly improving her profile. Her larger down payment also lowers the loan-to-value ratio, reducing lender risk.

Additionally, Olivia maintains $45,000 in reserves after closing, which covers approximately 14 months of mortgage payments. This further strengthens her file and provides reassurance to the lender.

From an underwriting perspective, Olivia's file has been transformed. What initially appeared to be a high-risk application is now a well-structured, balanced profile that demonstrates strong income, manageable debt, and financial stability. Olivia is approved for the loan with competitive terms, despite her credit challenges. The adjustments she made not only secured approval but also improved her long-term financial position. Her lower mortgage payment and reduced debt obligations provide greater financial flexibility moving forward.

This example highlights the power of strategic file structuring. By analyzing the numbers, identifying opportunities for improvement, and making targeted adjustments, borrowers can significantly enhance their chances of approval. It reinforces the idea that success in bank statement lending is not just about the numbers—it is about how those numbers are structured, presented, and aligned with lender expectations.

Chapter 5

Reducing Risk Through Strategic Borrower Positioning

In the world of bank statement mortgage loans, particularly when working with borrowers who have credit challenges, one of the most powerful concepts to understand is risk perception. Lending is fundamentally about risk management. Every decision made by a lender or underwriter revolves around one central question: how likely is this borrower to repay the loan as agreed? When a borrower has credit issues, the perceived risk naturally increases. However, what many borrowers and even loan professionals fail to realize is that risk is not fixed—it can be actively reduced through strategic positioning. This chapter focuses on how to reshape a borrower's profile in a way that lowers perceived risk and significantly improves the likelihood of approval.

Strategic borrower positioning begins with understanding how lenders think. Lenders are not looking for perfect borrowers; they are looking for predictable borrowers. Predictability comes from consistency, stability, and evidence of control over one's financial situation. When a borrower presents a profile that demonstrates these traits, the lender becomes more confident, even if there are imperfections in the credit history.

compelling case for approval. Consistent income, strong reserves, a solid down payment, reduced debt, and clear documentation all work together to lower perceived risk. The more of these elements that are present, the stronger the file becomes.

From a strategic standpoint, borrower positioning should begin well before the loan application. This preparation phase allows the borrower to make adjustments, strengthen weak areas, and optimize their profile. Waiting until the application is submitted is often too late to make meaningful changes. By planning ahead and taking a proactive approach, borrowers can significantly improve their chances of success.

Ultimately, reducing risk through strategic positioning is about control. While borrowers cannot change their past, they can control how their current financial situation is presented. By focusing on consistency, stability, and clarity, they can reshape the lender's perception and move from a position of risk to one of confidence.

This chapter reinforces a critical principle: approval is not just about meeting guidelines—it is about managing perception. When a borrower is positioned correctly, even significant credit challenges can be overcome. As you continue through this book, you will build on these strategies, learning how to refine and optimize every aspect of the loan process to achieve consistent and successful outcomes.

Real-Life Math Example: Reducing Risk Through Strategic Financial Adjustments

Let's explore a detailed real-world scenario involving a borrower named Marcus, a self-employed fitness coach who operates an online training business. Marcus has been in business for three years and generates strong income, but his credit score is 620 due to high credit card utilization and several late payments from two years ago. He is looking to purchase a home valued at $480,000.

Initially, Marcus plans to put down 15%, which equals $72,000. This results in a loan amount of $408,000. Over the past 12 months, Marcus has deposited $216,000 into his bank account, averaging $18,000 per month. The lender applies an expense factor of 50%, resulting in a qualifying monthly income of $9,000.

Marcus's current monthly debts total $2,700, including credit cards, a car loan, and a personal loan. The estimated monthly mortgage payment for his new home is $3,200, bringing his total monthly obligations to $5,900. Dividing $5,900 by $9,000 results in a debt-to-income ratio of approximately 66%, which is too high for most lenders. Recognizing the need to reduce risk, Marcus implements several strategic adjustments before applying. First, he pays down $12,000 in credit card debt, reducing his monthly obligations by $600. This lowers his total monthly debt from $5,900 to $5,300.

Next, Marcus increases his down payment from 15% to 20% by contributing an additional $24,000. This reduces his loan amount to $384,000 and lowers his monthly mortgage payment from $3,200 to $2,900. His total monthly obligations are now $5,000.

Marcus also works with his CPA to justify a lower expense factor of 40%, increasing his qualifying income from $9,000 to $10,800 per month. Recalculating his debt-to-income ratio, we divide $5,000 by $10,800, resulting in approximately 46%.

In addition to these changes, Marcus builds his reserves to $50,000, which covers approximately 17 months of mortgage payments. This significantly strengthens his profile and reduces perceived risk.

Let's compare the before-and-after scenarios. Initially, Marcus had a DTI of 66%, minimal reserves, and a lower down payment, making approval unlikely. After strategic adjustments, his DTI is reduced to 46%, his reserves are substantial, and his down payment is stronger. These changes transform his file from high risk to acceptable risk. From a financial perspective, the adjustments also improve Marcus's long-term position. His lower mortgage payment reduces monthly strain, and his reduced debt obligations provide greater flexibility. Additionally, his improved credit utilization leads to a slight increase in his credit score, further enhancing his profile.

Marcus is ultimately approved for the loan, despite his credit challenges. The interest rate is slightly higher than traditional loans, but the overall structure of the deal allows him to achieve homeownership while maintaining financial stability.

Let's quantify the impact of his adjustments. By reducing his monthly obligations from $5,900 to $5,000, Marcus saves $900 per month. Over a year, this equals $10,800 in improved cash flow. Over five years, this totals $54,000, demonstrating the long-term benefits of strategic positioning.

This example illustrates how borrowers can actively reduce risk and improve approval outcomes through thoughtful financial adjustments. By focusing on key variables—income, debt, down payment, and reserves—Marcus was able to transform his profile and secure financing. It reinforces the principle that success in bank statement lending is not just about qualification—it is about optimization and control.

Chapter 6

Lender Overlays, Investor Guidelines, and How to Choose the Right Program

As borrowers and loan professionals move deeper into the world of bank statement mortgage loans—especially when dealing with credit challenges—one of the most critical and often misunderstood components is the role of lender overlays and investor guidelines. Many borrowers assume that all bank statement loan programs are similar, but in reality, each lender operates within a unique framework of rules, tolerances, and risk preferences. Understanding these differences is essential for structuring successful deals, particularly when a borrower falls outside traditional credit standards.

At the core of this chapter is a simple but powerful truth: not all lenders evaluate risk the same way. While two lenders may both offer bank statement mortgage loans, their internal overlays—the additional guidelines layered on top of base program requirements—can vary significantly. These overlays determine how flexible or conservative a lender is when assessing credit challenges, income stability, reserves, and overall borrower strength. For borrowers with imperfect credit, selecting the right lender can mean the difference between approval and denial. Investor guidelines form the foundation of these programs. These guidelines are established by the institutions that ultimately fund or purchase the loans. They define baseline requirements such as minimum credit scores, acceptable seasoning for credit events, maximum debt-to-income ratios, and documentation standards. However, lenders often apply overlays to these guidelines to manage their own risk exposure. These overlays may tighten or expand the parameters, depending on the lender's appetite for certain types of loans.

For example, one lender may require a minimum credit score of 660 for a bank statement loan, while another may allow scores as low as 620 with strong compensating factors. Similarly, one lender may require two years of seasoning after a bankruptcy, while another may consider approvals after one year if the borrower demonstrates strong income and reserves. These differences create opportunities for strategic positioning, where the same borrower can qualify with one lender but not another.

Understanding overlays requires a shift in mindset. Instead of asking, "Do I qualify?" borrowers and professionals should ask, "Which lender am I best suited for?" This approach recognizes that qualification is not universal—it is program-specific. By identifying lenders whose guidelines align with the borrower's strengths, it becomes possible to navigate around limitations and maximize approval potential. One of the most important overlays to consider is credit tolerance. Some lenders are more forgiving of past credit events, while others place greater emphasis on recent payment history. For borrowers with credit challenges, it is essential to identify lenders that focus on current stability rather than past issues. These lenders often place greater weight on bank statement income, reserves, and overall financial behavior.

Another key area is debt-to-income flexibility. While traditional loans often have strict DTI limits, many bank statement programs allow higher ratios when supported by strong compensating factors. However, the extent of this flexibility varies by lender. Some may cap DTI at 50%, while others may allow up to 55% or even higher under specific conditions. Understanding these limits allows borrowers to structure their files accordingly and avoid unnecessary denials.

Reserve requirements are another critical factor. Lenders use reserves as a measure of financial stability, and their requirements can vary widely. Some programs may require six months of reserves, while others may require twelve or more, especially for borrowers with credit challenges. Choosing a lender whose reserve requirements align with the borrower's available assets can significantly improve approval chances.

Loan-to-value ratios also differ across programs. Borrowers with stronger credit profiles may qualify for higher LTVs, while those with credit challenges may be required to provide larger down payments. However, some lenders offer more flexibility in this area, allowing higher LTVs when other aspects of the file are strong. Understanding these nuances is essential for structuring the loan in a way that meets both the borrower's goals and the lender's guidelines.

Property type can also influence lender selection. Some lenders are more comfortable with investment properties, while others focus primarily on primary residences. Additionally, certain lenders may have restrictions on property types such as condos, multi-unit properties, or non-traditional assets. Matching the property to the right lender is an important part of the overall strategy.

Another important consideration is the documentation approach. While all bank statement loans rely on deposit analysis, some lenders may require additional documentation such as CPA-prepared profit and loss statements, business licenses, or letters of explanation. Others may offer more streamlined processes with fewer documentation requirements. Choosing a lender whose documentation standards align with the borrower's situation can simplify the process and reduce potential obstacles. Interest rates and pricing also vary between lenders, often reflecting their level of risk tolerance. Lenders with more flexible guidelines may offer higher interest rates to compensate for increased risk, while more conservative lenders may offer lower rates but stricter requirements. Understanding this trade-off allows borrowers to make informed decisions about whether to prioritize approval flexibility or pricing.

Timing is another strategic element when working with different lenders. Some programs may be more favorable during certain market conditions, while others may adjust their overlays based on economic trends. Staying informed about these changes allows borrowers and professionals to adapt their strategies and take advantage of favorable conditions.

Working with experienced loan professionals who understand the landscape of lender overlays is invaluable. These professionals can identify the best program for a specific borrower, anticipate potential challenges, and structure the file accordingly. Their knowledge of lender preferences and guidelines can significantly streamline the process and improve outcomes.

Ultimately, choosing the right lender is about alignment. It is about finding the program that best matches the borrower's financial profile, goals, and challenges. This alignment reduces friction in the underwriting process and increases the likelihood of approval. It transforms the loan process from a trial-and-error approach into a targeted, strategic effort. This chapter emphasizes that success in bank statement mortgage lending is not just about meeting requirements—it is about navigating options. By understanding lender overlays and investor guidelines, borrowers can position themselves more effectively, avoid unnecessary obstacles, and achieve approvals that might otherwise seem out of reach.

As you continue through this book, you will build on this knowledge, learning how to combine lender selection with strong file structuring, compensating factors, and strategic positioning to create consistent and successful outcomes.

Real-Life Math Example: Matching a Borrower to the Right Lender Program

Let's consider a detailed scenario involving a borrower named Isabella, a self-employed e-commerce business owner. Isabella has been in business for four years and generates strong revenue, but her credit score is 635 due to past late payments and high credit utilization. She is looking to purchase a property valued at $520,000.

Isabella plans to put down 20%, which equals $104,000,

resulting in a loan amount of $416,000. Over the past 12 months, she has deposited $300,000 into her business account, averaging $25,000 per month. The lender applies an expense factor of 50%, resulting in a qualifying monthly income of $12,500.

Her current monthly debts total $2,500, and the estimated mortgage payment for the property is $3,200. This brings her total monthly obligations to $5,700. Dividing $5,700 by $12,500 results in a debt-to-income ratio of approximately 46%.

At first glance, Isabella appears to be a strong candidate. However, the outcome depends heavily on the lender she chooses. Let's compare two different lender scenarios.

Lender A has stricter overlays. They require a minimum credit score of 660, a maximum DTI of 45%, and at least 12 months of reserves. Isabella does not meet the credit score requirement, and her DTI slightly exceeds the limit. As a result, she is denied by Lender A.

Lender B, on the other hand, has more flexible guidelines. They allow credit scores as low as 620 with strong compensating factors, a maximum DTI of 50%, and require only 6 months of reserves. Isabella meets all of these requirements. Additionally, she has $60,000 in reserves, which covers approximately 18 months of mortgage payments, far exceeding the minimum.

Now let's analyze the financial impact of choosing the right lender. Lender A offers a lower interest rate of 6.5%, while Lender B offers a rate of 7.25% due to the increased flexibility. The difference in rate affects Isabella's monthly payment.

At 6.5%, the estimated monthly payment would be approximately $2,630. At 7.25%, the payment increases to approximately $2,840. This is a difference of $210 per month.

Over one year, this difference equals $2,520. Over five years, it totals $12,600. While this is a higher cost, it must be weighed against the opportunity to secure the property.

Let's consider the broader financial picture. Isabella's property is expected to appreciate at an average rate of 4% per year. On a $520,000 property, this equates to $20,800 in appreciation during the first year alone. Over five years, this could exceed $100,000, depending on market conditions.

Additionally, Isabella's business income continues to grow, and she plans to refinance within two to three years once her credit improves. By doing so, she can secure a lower interest rate in the future, reducing her long-term costs.

Now let's compare the outcomes. If Isabella chooses Lender A, she is denied and misses the opportunity to purchase the property. If she chooses Lender B, she pays a higher interest rate initially but gains access to the property and its potential appreciation. Even with the higher interest cost of $12,600 over five years, the potential appreciation of over $100,000 far outweighs the additional expense. This demonstrates the importance of choosing the right lender and understanding the trade-offs involved.

This example highlights a critical lesson: approval is not just about numbers—it is about alignment. By selecting a lender whose guidelines match her profile, Isabella is able to achieve her goal despite her credit challenges. It reinforces the idea that in bank statement lending, strategy and lender selection are just as important as financial strength.

Chapter 7

Explaining Credit Events and Building a Compelling Borrower Narrative

In the world of bank statement mortgage loans—especially for borrowers with credit challenges—numbers alone are rarely enough to secure approval. While income, reserves, and debt ratios form the foundation of a loan file, there is another equally powerful element that often determines the outcome: the borrower's narrative. This narrative is the story behind the numbers, the explanation that provides context to credit events, and the bridge that connects past challenges to present stability. When crafted correctly, it can transform a file from questionable to compelling.

Underwriters are not only evaluating financial data; they are evaluating behavior, patterns, and risk. When they encounter negative credit events—such as late payments, collections, charge-offs, bankruptcies, or foreclosures—their natural response is to question the likelihood of recurrence. Without context, these events appear as red flags. However, when accompanied by a clear, logical, and well-documented explanation, those same events can be reframed as isolated incidents that have been resolved and are unlikely to happen again. The first step in building a strong borrower narrative is understanding the purpose of a letter of explanation. This document is not an excuse or a defense; it is a factual account of what happened, why it happened, and what has changed since then. It should be concise, professional, and focused on resolution. Overly emotional or lengthy explanations can dilute the message and reduce credibility. Instead, the goal is to provide clarity and reassurance.

A strong explanation typically follows a simple structure. First, it identifies the event and the timeframe. Second, it explains the cause in a clear and straightforward manner. Third, it outlines the actions taken to resolve the issue. Finally, it demonstrates evidence of stability and improvement since the event. This structure ensures that the underwriter can quickly understand the situation and assess the borrower's current risk profile.

For example, a borrower who experienced late payments due to a temporary business downturn might explain that a key client contract was lost, resulting in a short-term reduction in income. They would then describe how they secured new clients, stabilized their revenue, and have maintained consistent deposits and on-time payments since that period. When supported by bank statements and credit history, this explanation becomes a powerful tool in shifting the underwriter's perspective. Consistency between the narrative and the documentation is critical. If a borrower claims that their income has stabilized, the bank statements must reflect consistent deposits. If they state that debts have been reduced, the credit report must show lower balances. Any discrepancy between the explanation and the documentation can raise concerns and weaken the file. Therefore, the narrative must be aligned with the data at every level.

Another important aspect of the borrower narrative is timing. The more time that has passed since a credit event, the easier it is to demonstrate recovery and stability. However, even recent events can be explained effectively if the borrower can show immediate corrective action and strong current performance. The key is to focus on what has changed and why the situation is different now.

Patterns also play a significant role in how credit events are interpreted. A single isolated incident is generally easier to explain than a series of repeated issues. If multiple events have occurred, the narrative must address the underlying cause and demonstrate that it has been resolved. This may involve showing changes in business operations, financial management practices, or personal circumstances. The goal is to break the pattern and establish a new, stable trend.

Documentation supporting the narrative is equally important. This may include bank statements, profit and loss statements, business contracts, or other records that validate the explanation. For example, a borrower who experienced income disruption due to a temporary business closure can provide documentation showing the reopening of the business and subsequent revenue growth. This evidence reinforces the narrative and builds credibility.

Another powerful element of the borrower narrative is demonstrating financial maturity. This involves showing that the borrower has learned from past challenges and implemented strategies to prevent future issues. This could include maintaining higher reserves, reducing reliance on credit, or improving financial organization. These actions signal to the lender that the borrower is not only stable but also proactive in managing their finances.

It is also important to address potential concerns before they are raised. Anticipating the underwriter's questions and providing answers upfront can streamline the approval process and reduce the need for additional conditions. This proactive approach shows professionalism and confidence, which can positively influence the overall perception of the file.

The narrative should also be tailored to the specific lender and program. Different lenders may have different sensitivities to certain types of credit events. Understanding these preferences allows the borrower to emphasize the most relevant aspects of their story and align the narrative with the lender's priorities. This level of customization can significantly improve the effectiveness of the explanation.

From a strategic perspective, the borrower narrative is not just a reactive tool—it is a proactive one. It allows borrowers to take control of how their financial story is presented. Instead of allowing the credit report to speak for itself, the narrative provides context, clarity, and direction. It transforms the file from a collection of data points into a cohesive and persuasive case for approval.

Ultimately, the goal of the borrower narrative is to build trust. Lenders need to feel confident that the borrower is capable, reliable, and unlikely to repeat past mistakes. By presenting a clear, consistent, and well-supported story, borrowers can overcome credit challenges and position themselves as strong candidates for financing.

This chapter reinforces the idea that approval is not just about numbers—it is about perception. When the narrative is aligned with the data and supported by strong compensating factors, even complex credit histories can be successfully navigated. As you continue through this book, you will learn how to integrate this narrative approach with advanced structuring strategies to achieve consistent approvals.

Real-Life Math Example: Strengthening Approval Through Narrative and Financial Alignment

Let's consider a detailed scenario involving a borrower named Anthony, a self-employed restaurant owner. Anthony has been in business for five years and generates strong revenue, but his credit score is 630 due to a series of late payments and a temporary closure of his business two years ago. During that time, he struggled to meet his financial obligations, resulting in several negative marks on his credit report.

Anthony is now looking to purchase a home valued at $580,000. He plans to put down 20%, which equals $116,000, resulting in a loan amount of $464,000. Over the past 12 months, Anthony has deposited $360,000 into his business account, averaging $30,000 per month. The lender applies an expense factor of 50%, resulting in a qualifying monthly income of $15,000.

Anthony's current monthly debts total $3,000, including a car loan and remaining credit obligations. The estimated monthly mortgage payment for his new home is $3,500, bringing his total monthly obligations to $6,500. Dividing $6,500 by $15,000 results in a debt-to-income ratio of approximately 43%. From a numerical standpoint, Anthony's file appears strong. However, his credit history raises concerns due to the multiple late payments. This is where the borrower narrative becomes critical.

Anthony provides a clear and concise explanation of his situation. He explains that his restaurant was temporarily closed due to external circumstances, leading to a short-term loss of income. He details how he adapted by shifting to delivery services, securing new revenue streams, and eventually reopening with stronger operations. He also provides documentation showing consistent revenue growth over the past year.

Now let's analyze the financial impact of his recovery. During the downturn, Anthony's monthly income dropped to $10,000, while his obligations remained at $6,500, resulting in a DTI of 65%. This high ratio explains the late payments during that period.

However, after restructuring his business, his income increased to $30,000 per month in deposits, with a qualifying income of $15,000. His obligations remained at $6,500, reducing his DTI to 43%. This significant improvement demonstrates financial recovery and stability. Anthony also builds $70,000 in reserves, which covers approximately 20 months of mortgage payments. This further strengthens his profile and reduces perceived risk.

Let's quantify the strength of his current position. With a monthly income of $15,000 and obligations of $6,500, Anthony has $8,500 in remaining monthly cash flow. Over a year, this equals $102,000 in excess cash flow, providing a strong buffer against future challenges.

Additionally, Anthony's property is expected to appreciate at 4% annually. On a $580,000 property, this equates to $23,200 in the first year. Combined with his strong cash flow, this creates a solid financial foundation.

From an underwriting perspective, Anthony's narrative aligns perfectly with his financial data. His past challenges are clearly explained, his recovery is well-documented, and his current profile demonstrates stability and strength.

As a result, Anthony is approved for the loan, despite his credit challenges. The lender views his past issues as isolated and unlikely to recur, based on the strength of his narrative and financial performance.

This example illustrates how combining a strong borrower

narrative with solid financial metrics can transform a file. By aligning explanation with data and demonstrating clear recovery, Anthony was able to overcome credit challenges and achieve approval. It reinforces the principle that in bank statement lending, the story behind the numbers is just as important as the numbers themselves.

Chapter 8

Final Approval Strategies and Preparing for Underwriting Success

As borrowers and loan professionals reach the final stages of the bank statement mortgage process—especially when navigating credit challenges—the focus shifts from preparation to execution. At this stage, the difference between approval and delay, or even denial, often comes down to how well the file is finalized, presented, and managed through underwriting. Chapter 8 is dedicated to the final approval strategies that ensure a smooth transition from submission to closing, with an emphasis on precision, anticipation, and control.

Underwriting is not just a review process; it is a validation process. The underwriter's role is to confirm that every aspect of the file aligns with the lender's guidelines and risk tolerance. This includes verifying income calculations, reviewing bank statements, analyzing credit history, confirming assets, and ensuring that all documentation is complete and consistent. For borrowers with credit challenges, this stage requires an even higher level of attention to detail, as the file must withstand closer scrutiny. The first and most critical step in preparing for underwriting success is conducting a pre-underwriting review. This involves analyzing the file as if you were the underwriter, identifying potential issues, and resolving them before submission. Common areas of concern include inconsistent bank deposits, unexplained large transactions, recent credit inquiries, and gaps in documentation. By addressing these issues proactively, borrowers can reduce the likelihood of conditions and create a smoother underwriting experience.

Bank statement analysis remains a central component at this stage. Underwriters will closely examine deposit patterns, looking for consistency and eligibility. Any large or irregular deposits must be explained and documented. Transfers between accounts, one-time payments, or unusual activity can raise questions if not clearly identified. A well-prepared file includes labeled statements, clear summaries, and supporting documentation that eliminates ambiguity.

Income calculation must also be precise and defensible. The expense factor applied to bank statement deposits should be supported by documentation, such as a CPA-prepared profit and loss statement when applicable. Any discrepancies between stated income and documented deposits can lead to conditions or recalculations. Ensuring that income is calculated accurately from the beginning helps prevent delays and maintains the integrity of the file. Credit review at the underwriting stage focuses heavily on recent activity. While past credit events may already be accounted for, underwriters will look for any new issues that could indicate increased risk. This includes recent late payments, new accounts, or significant changes in credit utilization. Borrowers should maintain strict discipline during this period, avoiding new debt and ensuring all payments are made on time.

Asset verification is another key component. Underwriters will confirm that funds used for the down payment and reserves are properly sourced and seasoned. Large deposits into asset accounts may require documentation to verify their origin. Ensuring that assets are organized and clearly documented reduces the likelihood of additional conditions and expedites the approval process.

One of the most important strategies for final approval is anticipating conditions. Conditions are requests from the underwriter for additional information or clarification. While some conditions are unavoidable, many can be predicted and addressed in advance. For example, if there are large deposits in the bank statements, providing explanations and documentation upfront can eliminate the need for a condition. This proactive approach demonstrates professionalism and reduces turnaround time.

Communication during underwriting is also critical. Timely responses to conditions, clear documentation, and consistent follow-up help keep the file moving forward. Delays in responding to requests can slow down the process and create unnecessary complications. Maintaining open and efficient communication ensures that the file progresses smoothly toward approval.

Another key factor is maintaining financial stability throughout the underwriting process. Borrowers should avoid any changes that could impact their profile, such as switching jobs, altering business operations, or making large financial transactions. Stability is essential during this phase, as any significant changes can trigger additional review or even jeopardize the approval.

Property-related factors must also be considered. The appraisal, title, and insurance requirements all play a role in final approval. Ensuring that the property meets lender guidelines and that all related documentation is in place is essential. Any issues with the property can delay closing or require additional conditions.

Final approval is often followed by a clear-to-close status, which indicates that all conditions have been satisfied and the loan is ready to proceed to closing. Reaching this stage requires careful coordination of all elements within the file. Every detail must align, and every requirement must be met. Closing preparation is the final step in the process. This includes reviewing closing disclosures, confirming final numbers, and ensuring that funds are ready for transfer. Borrowers should be fully prepared for this stage, with all necessary documentation and funds in place. A smooth closing is the result of thorough preparation and attention to detail throughout the entire process.

Ultimately, final approval strategies are about precision and control. While earlier stages focus on building and strengthening the file, this stage focuses on executing the plan flawlessly. Every detail matters, and every step must be managed carefully.

This chapter reinforces the importance of preparation, anticipation, and discipline. By approaching underwriting with a proactive mindset and a well-structured file, borrowers can navigate the final stages with confidence and efficiency. For those with credit challenges, this level of preparation is not just beneficial—it is essential.

As you move toward the final chapters of this book, you will continue to refine these strategies, gaining the knowledge and confidence needed to consistently achieve successful outcomes in the bank statement mortgage loan process.

Real-Life Math Example: Finalizing Approval Through Strategic Execution

Let's examine a detailed scenario involving a borrower named Rachel, a self-employed consultant with strong income but a credit score of 640 due to past late payments. Rachel is purchasing a home valued at $620,000 and plans to put down 20%, or $124,000, resulting in a loan amount of $496,000.

Over the past 12 months, Rachel has deposited $360,000 into her bank account, averaging $30,000 per month. The lender applies an expense factor of 50%, resulting in a qualifying monthly income of $15,000.

Rachel's monthly debts total $3,500, and the estimated mortgage payment is $3,800. This brings her total monthly obligations to $7,300. Dividing $7,300 by $15,000 results in a debt-to-income ratio of approximately 49%, which is within acceptable guidelines.

During pre-underwriting review, Rachel identifies a potential issue: several large deposits totaling $50,000 that are not part of her regular income. These deposits are from a one-time consulting project. Without explanation, these could be excluded from income or raise questions.

Rachel provides documentation showing the source of these funds, including contracts and invoices. She also clarifies that these deposits are not part of her recurring income. This proactive step prevents conditions and ensures accurate income calculation.

Now let's analyze the financial impact of her preparation. Without proper documentation, the lender might exclude these deposits and question her income stability. However, by clearly identifying them as non-recurring, Rachel maintains the integrity of her income calculation at $15,000 per month.

Rachel also ensures that her assets are properly documented. She has $80,000 in reserves after closing, which covers approximately 21 months of mortgage payments. This strong reserve position enhances her profile and reduces perceived risk.

During underwriting, Rachel receives a condition requesting confirmation of her business stability. She responds promptly with updated bank statements and a letter from her CPA confirming consistent income. This quick response keeps the file moving forward.

Let's quantify Rachel's financial position. With a monthly income of $15,000 and obligations of $7,300, she has $7,700 in remaining cash flow each month. Over a year, this equals

$92,400 in excess cash flow, providing a strong financial buffer. Additionally, her property is expected to appreciate at 4% annually, equating to $24,800 in the first year. Combined with her cash flow, this creates a solid financial outlook.

Rachel's careful preparation and proactive approach result in a smooth underwriting process. She receives final approval and clear-to-close status without significant delays.

This example demonstrates how attention to detail and strategic execution can make a significant difference in the final stages of the loan process. By anticipating issues, providing clear documentation, and maintaining financial stability, Rachel successfully navigates underwriting and achieves approval despite her credit challenges.

It reinforces the principle that final approval is not just about qualification—it is about execution. When every detail is managed correctly, the path to closing becomes clear and achievable.

Chapter 9

Interest Rates, Risk-Based Pricing, and Long-Term Strategy

As borrowers with credit challenges navigate the bank statement mortgage loan process, one of the most important realities they must understand is the concept of risk-based pricing. Unlike traditional lending, where borrowers with strong credit profiles receive the most favorable terms, bank statement mortgage loans operate within a flexible framework where pricing reflects perceived risk. This means that interest rates are not simply based on market conditions—they are directly influenced by the borrower's overall financial profile, including credit history, income stability, reserves, and loan structure.

For many borrowers, especially those who have faced credit challenges, the initial reaction to a higher interest rate is hesitation. However, it is critical to reframe this perspective. The purpose of bank statement lending is not necessarily to provide the lowest possible rate at the outset, but to provide access to financing when traditional options are unavailable. In this sense, the loan becomes a strategic tool—a stepping stone that allows the borrower to achieve their goals now, while positioning themselves for improved terms in the future.

To fully understand this concept, it is important to break down how risk-based pricing works. Lenders evaluate multiple factors when determining an interest rate. Credit score is one of the primary components, with lower scores typically resulting in higher rates. However, it is not the only factor. Loan-to-value ratio, debt-to-income ratio, reserve levels, property type, and overall file strength all contribute to the final pricing. A borrower with a lower credit score but strong compensating factors may receive a more favorable rate than expected, while a borrower with weaker overall metrics may face higher pricing.

Loan-to-value ratio, or LTV, plays a particularly significant role. A lower LTV—achieved through a larger down payment—reduces the lender's risk and can result in better pricing. For example, a borrower putting down 25% or 30% may receive a noticeably lower rate than one putting down only 10% or 15%. This creates an opportunity for borrowers to actively influence their rate by adjusting their down payment strategy.

Debt-to-income ratio also impacts pricing. Borrowers with lower DTIs are generally viewed as less risky, as they have more available income to cover their obligations. By reducing debt or increasing qualifying income, borrowers can improve their DTI and potentially secure better terms. This highlights the importance of structuring the file not just for approval, but for optimal pricing. Reserves provide another layer of influence. Borrowers with substantial reserves demonstrate financial stability and the ability to weather unexpected challenges. This reduces perceived risk and can positively impact pricing. In many cases, increasing reserves by even a few months of mortgage payments can lead to improved loan terms.

Property type is also a factor. Primary residences typically receive more favorable pricing than investment properties, as they are considered lower risk. However, even within investment properties, factors such as location, rental potential, and borrower experience can influence how the lender evaluates risk.

Understanding these variables allows borrowers to approach the loan process strategically. Instead of passively accepting a rate, they can actively shape their profile to achieve better terms. This may involve increasing the down payment, reducing debt, or strengthening reserves prior to applying.

Another critical concept is the long-term strategy behind accepting a higher initial rate. For many borrowers with credit challenges, the bank statement loan is not the final destination—it is the first step. By securing financing now, the borrower gains access to property ownership, potential appreciation, and the opportunity to build equity. At the same time, they can work on improving their credit profile, reducing debt, and strengthening their financial position.

Refinancing becomes a key component of this strategy. Once the borrower's credit improves and their financial profile strengthens, they can refinance into a lower-rate loan. This transition allows them to reduce their monthly payment and long-term interest costs. The initial higher rate is therefore temporary, serving as a bridge to a more favorable position.

Timing the refinance is essential. Borrowers should monitor their credit, income, and market conditions to determine the optimal moment to refinance. Waiting too long may result in unnecessary interest costs, while refinancing too early may limit the benefits. A well-timed refinance can significantly enhance the overall financial outcome.

It is also important to consider the cost of waiting versus the cost of acting. Many borrowers delay purchasing or refinancing due to concerns about higher interest rates. However, this delay can result in missed opportunities, particularly in appreciating markets. The potential increase in property value, combined with the benefits of ownership, may outweigh the additional cost of a higher rate.

Cash flow analysis plays a crucial role in this decision-making process. Borrowers must evaluate whether the loan structure allows them to maintain positive or manageable cash flow. Even with a higher rate, a well-structured loan can provide financial stability and support long-term goals.

Another strategic consideration is the use of additional income or savings to offset higher costs. For example, borrowers may choose to make extra payments toward principal, reducing the overall interest paid over time. This proactive approach can mitigate the impact of a higher rate and accelerate equity growth.

It is also worth noting that interest rates are influenced by broader economic conditions. Market trends, inflation, and monetary policy all play a role in determining rates. While borrowers cannot control these factors, they can control how they respond to them. By focusing on what can be managed—such as credit improvement and financial positioning—they can navigate changing conditions effectively.

Ultimately, risk-based pricing is not a barrier—it is a framework. It reflects the lender's assessment of risk and provides a pathway for borrowers to access financing. By understanding how this framework works, borrowers can make informed decisions, optimize their loan structure, and develop a clear long-term strategy.

This chapter emphasizes that success in bank statement mortgage lending is not just about securing approval—it is about maximizing opportunity. By viewing the loan as part of a broader financial plan, borrowers can turn short-term challenges into long-term advantages.

As you move into the final chapter of this book, you will bring together all the concepts discussed so far, creating a complete and actionable strategy for achieving consistent success in bank statement mortgage loans, regardless of credit challenges.

Real-Life Math Example: Evaluating Interest Rates and Long-Term Strategy

Let's consider a detailed scenario involving a borrower named David, a self-employed consultant with a credit score of 630. David is purchasing a home valued at $600,000 and plans to put down 20%, or $120,000, resulting in a loan amount of $480,000.

David's lender offers him a bank statement loan with an interest rate of 7.5%. If David had a higher credit score, he might qualify for a rate of 6.5%. The difference in rate has a direct impact on his monthly payment.

At 7.5%, David's monthly mortgage payment is approximately $3,356. At 6.5%, the payment would be approximately $3,034. This is a difference of $322 per month. Over one year, this difference equals $3,864. Over five years, it totals $19,320. At first glance, this additional cost may seem significant. However, it is important to consider the broader financial picture.

David's property is expected to appreciate at an average rate of 4% per year. On a $600,000 property, this equates to $24,000 in the first year. Over five years, this could exceed $120,000, depending on market conditions.

Additionally, David's income continues to grow, and he plans to refinance within three years once his credit improves. Let's assume he refinances into a 6.5% rate at that time. By doing so, he reduces his monthly payment by $322 moving forward.

Let's calculate the cost before refinancing. Over three years, the additional cost of the higher rate is $11,592. After refinancing, David benefits from the lower rate, reducing his monthly expenses.

Now let's compare this cost to the benefits. Over three years, David's property may appreciate by approximately $72,000. Even after accounting for the additional interest cost, he still gains significant equity.

Additionally, David benefits from three years of homeownership, including potential tax advantages and the stability of owning his property. These benefits further enhance the overall value of the decision. David also has the option to make additional principal payments. If he pays an extra $200 per month toward principal, he reduces his loan balance faster and decreases the total interest paid over time. Over three years, this adds up to $7,200 in additional principal reduction.

When we combine appreciation, principal reduction, and the strategic refinance, David's overall financial position improves significantly. The initial higher rate becomes a temporary cost rather than a long-term burden.

This example demonstrates the importance of viewing interest rates within the context of a broader strategy. While risk-based pricing may result in higher initial costs, it also provides access to opportunities that can generate long-term value.

By understanding the numbers and planning strategically, borrowers like David can make informed decisions that align with their goals. It reinforces the idea that in bank statement lending, success is not defined by the initial rate—it is defined by the overall outcome.

Chapter 10

Mastering the System—From Credit Challenges to Consistent Mortgage Approvals

As we reach the final chapter of *The Bank Statement Mortgage Loan Mastery Series: Book 9*, it is time to bring together every concept, strategy, and principle discussed throughout this book into one unified approach. This chapter is not about introducing new ideas, but about mastering the system—understanding how all the moving parts work together to consistently achieve mortgage approvals, even for borrowers with credit challenges. By this point, it should be clear that approval is not about perfection. It is about preparation, positioning, structure, and execution.

The journey begins with a shift in mindset. Borrowers with credit challenges often believe they are at a disadvantage, but in reality, they are simply operating within a different framework. Bank statement mortgage loans are designed to evaluate the borrower as a whole, rather than relying solely on traditional metrics. This creates an opportunity to succeed by focusing on what can be controlled: income presentation, asset positioning, debt management, and strategic planning. The first pillar of mastering the system is understanding your financial story. Every borrower has a unique profile, shaped by their income, business activity, credit history, and financial decisions. The key is to identify the strengths within that profile and build around them. Strong bank statement deposits, consistent income, and liquidity are often the foundation. Even if credit challenges exist, these strengths can be leveraged to create a compelling case for approval.

The second pillar is structuring the file strategically. As discussed in earlier chapters, the way a loan is presented can significantly influence the outcome. This includes organizing bank statements, applying the appropriate expense factor, managing debt-to-income ratios, and positioning assets effectively. A well-structured file does more than meet guidelines—it tells a clear and convincing story that aligns with lender expectations.

The third pillar is leveraging compensating factors. These factors act as the balance within the file, offsetting weaknesses and reducing perceived risk. Strong reserves, larger down payments, stable business operations, and consistent deposit patterns all contribute to a stronger profile. The goal is to create a combination of strengths that outweigh any concerns related to credit history. The fourth pillar is understanding and navigating lender overlays. As explored in Chapter 6, not all lenders operate under the same guidelines. Choosing the right lender is a strategic decision that can determine the success of the application. By aligning the borrower's profile with the appropriate program, it is possible to achieve approvals that might not be available elsewhere.

The fifth pillar is timing. Knowing when to apply is just as important as how to apply. Waiting for the right moment—when income is stable, credit is improving, and assets are well-positioned—can significantly enhance the chances of approval. Strategic timing allows borrowers to present the strongest version of their financial profile.

The sixth pillar is execution during underwriting. This stage requires precision, discipline, and responsiveness. Anticipating conditions, providing clear documentation, and maintaining financial stability throughout the process are essential for achieving final approval. Every detail matters, and a proactive approach can prevent delays and complications.

The seventh and final pillar is long-term strategy. Bank statement mortgage loans are not just about obtaining financing—they are about building a pathway to financial growth. This includes planning for future refinancing, improving credit over time, and leveraging property ownership to create wealth. By viewing the loan as part of a broader strategy, borrowers can maximize the benefits and minimize the costs.

When these pillars are combined, they form a comprehensive system for achieving consistent mortgage approvals. This system is not dependent on perfect credit or ideal circumstances. Instead, it is built on knowledge, preparation, and strategic action. It empowers borrowers to take control of their financial journey and navigate challenges with confidence.

One of the most important lessons in mastering this system is adaptability. Every borrower's situation is different, and every loan presents unique challenges. The ability to adjust strategies, explore different options, and respond to changing conditions is essential. Flexibility allows borrowers to overcome obstacles and find solutions where others may see limitations.

Another key element is persistence. Mortgage approval, especially in complex scenarios, may require multiple attempts or adjustments. A denial is not the end of the process—it is feedback. By analyzing the reasons for denial and making targeted improvements, borrowers can strengthen their profile and try again with a higher likelihood of success.

Education also plays a critical role. Understanding how the system works—how income is calculated, how credit is evaluated, how lenders assess risk—provides a significant advantage. Knowledge allows borrowers to make informed decisions, avoid common mistakes, and approach the process with confidence.

It is also important to recognize the role of professional guidance. Experienced loan officers, brokers, and financial advisors can provide valuable insights and help navigate complex situations. Their expertise can streamline the process, identify opportunities, and ensure that the file is structured effectively.

As this book concludes, the overarching message is clear: credit challenges do not define your future. They are part of your financial history, but they do not determine your potential. With the right strategies, preparation, and mindset, it is possible to achieve mortgage approval and move forward with confidence.

The bank statement mortgage loan system is not just an alternative—it is an opportunity. It allows borrowers to demonstrate their true financial capability, beyond the limitations of traditional metrics. It provides a pathway to homeownership, investment, and long-term wealth creation.

By mastering this system, you gain more than just the ability to secure a loan. You gain control over your financial journey. You gain the knowledge to navigate challenges and the confidence to pursue opportunities. Most importantly, you gain the ability to turn obstacles into stepping stones toward success.

This is not the end of the journey—it is the beginning of a new chapter. Armed with the knowledge and strategies from this book, you are now equipped to approach the mortgage process with clarity, confidence, and purpose. The path forward is yours to create.

Real-Life Math Example: Building a Complete Approval Strategy from Start to Finish

Let's bring everything together with a comprehensive real-life scenario involving a borrower named Elena, a self-employed digital marketing consultant. Elena has a credit score of 635 due to past late payments and high credit utilization, but she has strong income and is determined to purchase a home valued at $650,000.

Elena plans to put down 20%, which equals $130,000, resulting in a loan amount of $520,000. Over the past 12 months, she has deposited $420,000 into her bank account, averaging $35,000 per month. The lender applies an expense factor of 50%, resulting in a qualifying monthly income of $17,500.

Her current monthly debts total $4,000, including credit cards and a car loan. The estimated mortgage payment is $4,000, bringing her total monthly obligations to $8,000. Dividing $8,000 by $17,500 results in a debt-to-income ratio of approximately 46%.

Initially, Elena's file is borderline due to her credit score and DTI. However, she implements a comprehensive strategy to strengthen her profile.

First, she pays down $15,000 in credit card debt, reducing her monthly obligations by $500. This lowers her total monthly debt to $7,500. Recalculating her DTI, we divide $7,500 by $17,500, resulting in approximately 43%.

Next, Elena works with her CPA to justify a lower expense factor of 40%, increasing her qualifying income to $21,000 per month. Dividing $7,500 by $21,000 results in a new DTI of approximately 36%.

Elena also increases her reserves to $80,000, which covers 20 months of mortgage payments. This significantly strengthens her file and reduces perceived risk.

Now let's analyze the financial impact of her strategy. With a monthly income of $21,000 and obligations of $7,500, Elena has $13,500 in remaining cash flow each month. Over a year, this equals $162,000 in excess cash flow.

Elena is approved for the loan with an interest rate of 7.25%. If her credit were higher, she might qualify for a rate of 6.5%, resulting in a monthly payment difference of approximately $350.

Over three years, this additional cost totals $12,600. However, Elena's property is expected to appreciate at 4% annually, equating to $26,000 in the first year and approximately $78,000 over three years.

Additionally, Elena plans to refinance after two years once her credit improves. By doing so, she reduces her monthly payment and long-term interest costs.

Let's combine the numbers. Over two years, the additional interest cost is approximately $8,400. However, the property may appreciate by over $52,000 during that time. Even after accounting for the higher rate, Elena gains significant equity.

Elena also chooses to make an extra $300 monthly payment toward principal. Over two years, this adds up to $7,200 in additional principal reduction, further improving her financial position.

When we combine appreciation, principal reduction, and strategic refinancing, Elena's overall outcome is highly positive. The initial challenges related to credit are outweighed by the long-term benefits of ownership and financial growth. This example demonstrates the power of mastering the system. By combining income optimization, debt reduction, strategic structuring, and long-term planning, Elena transforms a challenging file into a successful approval.

It reinforces the core principle of this book: success is not about perfection—it is about strategy. When all elements are aligned and executed correctly, borrowers can achieve consistent approvals and build a strong financial future, regardless of past credit challenges.

Chapter 11

Scaling Approvals—From One Loan to a Repeatable System

Once a borrower or loan professional successfully navigates a bank statement mortgage loan with credit challenges, the next level of mastery is not just achieving one approval—but creating a repeatable system that produces consistent results. Chapter 11 focuses on scaling success. Whether the goal is to acquire multiple properties, grow a real estate portfolio, or build a business around originating these loans, the principles in this chapter will help transform a one-time approval into a long-term strategy.

The first step in scaling approvals is recognizing that every successful loan contains a pattern. That pattern includes how income was structured, how credit challenges were explained, how compensating factors were used, and how the file was presented to the lender. By identifying and documenting these elements, borrowers and professionals can replicate what worked and refine what did not. This transforms the process from trial-and-error into a systematic approach.

For borrowers, especially investors, scaling begins with consistency in financial behavior. Lenders favor predictability, and borrowers who maintain consistent deposit patterns, stable business income, and disciplined financial management create a foundation for multiple approvals. This means avoiding unnecessary fluctuations in income, maintaining organized financial records, and ensuring that each loan builds upon the strength of the previous one.

One of the most important strategies for scaling is managing liquidity across multiple transactions. Each loan requires down payments, reserves, and closing costs, so it is essential to plan how capital will be allocated. Borrowers must balance the desire to acquire additional properties with the need to maintain sufficient reserves. This requires careful planning and a clear understanding of how each transaction impacts overall financial strength.

Another key element is leveraging equity from existing properties. As properties appreciate and loan balances decrease, borrowers can access equity through refinancing or lines of credit. This equity can then be used to fund additional purchases, creating a cycle of growth. However, this strategy must be approached carefully to avoid over-leveraging. Maintaining a healthy balance between equity and debt is critical for long-term stability. Credit management becomes even more important when scaling approvals. Each new loan impacts the borrower's credit profile, including inquiries, new accounts, and overall utilization. Borrowers must be strategic about when and how they apply for additional financing, ensuring that their credit profile remains strong enough to support future approvals. This may involve spacing out applications, paying down debt between transactions, and monitoring credit activity closely.

Income scalability is another critical factor. Lenders will evaluate whether the borrower's income can support multiple properties and increased debt obligations. This means demonstrating growth or stability in business income, as well as ensuring that bank statement deposits reflect the ability to handle additional loans. For self-employed borrowers, this may involve expanding operations, diversifying income streams, or optimizing pricing and revenue models.

Another powerful concept in scaling is standardization. By creating a consistent process for organizing documents, analyzing income, and structuring files, borrowers and professionals can streamline the approval process. This includes maintaining updated bank statements, tracking deposit patterns, preparing explanations in advance, and keeping all financial records organized. Standardization reduces errors, saves time, and improves efficiency. For loan professionals, scaling approvals involves building relationships with multiple lenders and understanding their unique guidelines. By knowing which lenders are best suited for different scenarios, professionals can match borrowers with the right programs more effectively. This not only increases approval rates but also builds a reputation for reliability and expertise.

Timing also plays a crucial role in scaling. Borrowers must be strategic about when they pursue additional loans, ensuring that their financial profile is strong enough to support each new transaction. This may involve waiting for income to stabilize, reserves to increase, or credit to improve before moving forward. Patience and planning are essential for sustainable growth.

Risk management becomes increasingly important as the number of properties grows. Each additional loan increases exposure, so borrowers must ensure that their portfolio remains balanced and manageable. This includes maintaining positive cash flow, monitoring market conditions, and avoiding excessive leverage. A well-managed portfolio not only supports future approvals but also provides long-term financial security.

Another key strategy is reinvesting profits. Rental income, business revenue, and property appreciation can all be reinvested to fuel further growth. By allocating profits strategically, borrowers can accelerate their progress and expand their portfolio more efficiently. This creates a cycle of growth where each success builds upon the previous one.

Documentation discipline is also essential when scaling. As the number of transactions increases, so does the complexity of financial records. Maintaining accurate and organized documentation ensures that each new loan can be processed smoothly. This includes keeping track of income, expenses, assets, and liabilities across all properties and accounts.

One of the most powerful aspects of scaling is momentum. Once a borrower establishes a track record of successful approvals, lenders become more confident in their ability to manage additional loans. This can lead to more favorable terms, faster approvals, and greater flexibility. Momentum builds trust, and trust opens doors.

It is also important to recognize the role of long-term vision. Scaling approvals is not just about acquiring more properties—it is about building a sustainable and profitable portfolio. This requires setting clear goals, developing a strategy, and staying focused on long-term outcomes rather than short-term gains.

Ultimately, scaling approvals is about turning knowledge into action. It is about applying the principles learned throughout this book in a consistent and disciplined manner. By doing so, borrowers and professionals can move beyond individual transactions and create a system that generates ongoing success.

This chapter reinforces the idea that success in bank statement mortgage lending is not limited to a single approval. With the right strategies, it can be expanded into a repeatable process that supports long-term growth and financial independence.

Real-Life Math Example: Scaling from One Property to a Portfolio

Let's examine a comprehensive scenario involving a borrower named Victor, a self-employed real estate consultant who successfully secured his first bank statement mortgage loan despite a credit score of 640. After his initial success, Victor wants to scale his strategy and build a portfolio of investment properties.

Victor's first property is valued at $500,000. He put down 20%, or $100,000, resulting in a loan amount of $400,000. The property generates $3,500 per month in rental income, while his mortgage payment is $2,800, resulting in a positive cash flow of $700 per month.

Over one year, this property generates $8,400 in net income. Additionally, the property appreciates at 4%, increasing its value by $20,000. Combined, Victor gains $28,400 in financial benefit from his first property in the first year.

Now let's analyze how Victor scales to a second property. After one year, Victor has saved $50,000 from his business income and rental cash flow. He also refinances his first property, accessing $40,000 in equity due to appreciation. This gives him a total of $90,000 for his next investment.

Victor purchases a second property valued at $450,000, putting down 20%, or $90,000. The loan amount is $360,000. This property generates $3,200 per month in rental income, with a mortgage payment of $2,600, resulting in a positive cash flow of $600 per month.

Now Victor has two properties generating a combined monthly cash flow of $1,300. Over a year, this equals $15,600 in net income. Both properties also appreciate at 4%, adding approximately $38,000 in combined value.

After another year, Victor repeats the process. He saves additional income, leverages equity, and acquires a third property valued at $400,000 with a $80,000 down payment. This property generates $2,800 per month in rental income with a $2,300 payment, producing $500 in monthly cash flow.

At this point, Victor's portfolio includes three properties with a combined monthly cash flow of $1,800, or $21,600 annually. The total value of his properties is now $1,350,000, and annual appreciation at 4% adds $54,000 in value.

Let's summarize Victor's growth over three years. He started with one property and scaled to three, generating over $21,600 in annual cash flow and $54,000 in annual appreciation. His total financial benefit exceeds $75,000 per year.

Even if Victor's initial loans carried slightly higher interest rates due to his credit challenges, the overall financial outcome is highly positive. The combination of cash flow, appreciation, and equity growth far outweighs the additional interest costs.

This example demonstrates how a single approval can evolve into a scalable system. By reinvesting profits, leveraging equity, and maintaining financial discipline, Victor transforms his initial success into a growing portfolio.

It reinforces the principle that bank statement mortgage loans are not just a solution for one transaction—they are a tool for building long-term wealth. When applied strategically, they can create a repeatable path to financial growth, even for borrowers with credit challenges.

Chapter 12

Long-Term Wealth Building and Exit Strategies Using Bank Statement Mortgage Loans

As we reach the final chapter of this book, the focus shifts from approval and acquisition to long-term wealth building and strategic exits. While securing a bank statement mortgage loan—especially with credit challenges—is a major accomplishment, it is only the beginning of a much larger financial journey. The true power of these loans lies in how they are used over time to create equity, generate income, and ultimately provide financial freedom. Chapter 12 is about understanding how to turn access into advantage and how to build a sustainable, long-term strategy that extends far beyond a single loan.

The first concept to understand is that real estate is not just an expense—it is an asset. When structured correctly, a property can generate income, appreciate in value, and serve as a foundation for future opportunities. Bank statement mortgage loans provide access to this asset class for borrowers who may not qualify through traditional channels. Once that access is secured, the focus must shift to maximizing the value of each property.

Equity is one of the most powerful tools in real estate wealth building. Equity represents the difference between the property's value and the remaining loan balance. As the property appreciates and the loan is paid down, equity increases. This equity can be leveraged to acquire additional properties, fund investments, or provide financial flexibility. Understanding how to build and use equity is essential for long-term success.

Cash flow is another critical component. A property that generates positive cash flow provides ongoing income that can be reinvested or used to support other financial goals. Even properties with minimal cash flow can become valuable over time as rents increase and loan balances decrease. The key is to ensure that each property is structured in a way that supports sustainability and growth.

One of the most effective strategies for long-term wealth building is the "buy, improve, and refinance" approach. This involves acquiring a property, increasing its value through improvements or market appreciation, and then refinancing to access the increased equity. The funds obtained from refinancing can then be used to acquire additional properties, creating a cycle of growth. This strategy is particularly powerful when combined with bank statement loans, as it allows borrowers to continue expanding even if their income is not documented through traditional means.

Refinancing plays a central role in long-term strategy. As credit improves and financial profiles strengthen, borrowers can transition from higher-rate bank statement loans to lower-rate traditional loans. This reduces monthly payments, increases cash flow, and improves overall profitability. Timing the refinance correctly is essential, as it allows borrowers to maximize the benefits while minimizing costs.

Another important strategy is diversification. While real estate can be a powerful wealth-building tool, relying solely on one type of property or market can increase risk. Diversifying across different property types, locations, or income streams can provide stability and reduce exposure to market fluctuations. For example, combining residential properties with short-term rentals or multi-family units can create a more balanced portfolio.

Exit strategies are equally important in long-term planning. An exit strategy defines how and when a property will be sold, refinanced, or transitioned to another use. Having a clear exit plan ensures that decisions are made strategically rather than reactively. Common exit strategies include selling properties after appreciation, refinancing to reduce costs, or holding properties for long-term income and legacy building.

Market awareness is a key factor in determining exit timing. Understanding local market trends, property values, and economic conditions allows borrowers to make informed decisions about when to buy, hold, or sell. While it is impossible to predict the market perfectly, staying informed and adaptable can significantly improve outcomes.

Tax strategy also plays a role in wealth building. Real estate offers various tax advantages, including deductions for mortgage interest, property taxes, and depreciation. Understanding how these benefits impact overall financial performance can enhance profitability and support long-term growth. Working with tax professionals can help optimize these strategies and ensure compliance.

Risk management remains essential throughout the process. As portfolios grow, so does exposure to potential challenges such as market downturns, vacancies, or unexpected expenses. Maintaining reserves, monitoring cash flow, and avoiding over-leverage are critical for long-term stability. A well-managed portfolio is not just profitable—it is resilient.

Another key concept is legacy building. Real estate can serve as a foundation for generational wealth, providing income and assets that can be passed down over time. By structuring investments with a long-term perspective, borrowers can create opportunities not only for themselves but also for future generations.

It is also important to recognize the role of discipline. Wealth building is not achieved through a single transaction or short-term gain. It requires consistent effort, strategic planning, and the ability to stay focused on long-term goals. Each decision—from property selection to financing—should align with the overall strategy.

Technology and data can also support long-term success. Tracking performance metrics, analyzing cash flow, and monitoring market trends allow borrowers to make informed decisions and optimize their portfolio. This data-driven approach enhances efficiency and improves outcomes.

Ultimately, the goal of this chapter is to shift the perspective from short-term approval to long-term opportunity. Bank statement mortgage loans are not just a solution for overcoming credit challenges—they are a gateway to building wealth. By applying the strategies outlined in this chapter, borrowers can transform access into advantage and create a sustainable path to financial success. As this book concludes, the message is clear: the journey does not end with approval. It begins there. With the knowledge and strategies you have gained, you are now equipped to move forward with confidence, build a strong financial foundation, and create opportunities that extend far beyond a single loan.

Real-Life Math Example: Building Long-Term Wealth Through Strategic Real Estate Growth

Let's consider a comprehensive scenario involving a borrower named Sofia, a self-employed entrepreneur who used a bank statement mortgage loan to purchase her first property despite a credit score of 640. Sofia's goal is not just to own one property, but to build long-term wealth through strategic growth.

Sofia's first property is valued at $550,000. She puts down 20%, or $110,000, resulting in a loan amount of $440,000. The property generates $3,800 per month in rental income, while her mortgage payment is $3,000, resulting in a positive cash flow of $800 per month.

Over one year, Sofia earns $9,600 in net rental income. Additionally, the property appreciates at 4%, increasing its value by $22,000. Combined, this results in a total financial gain of $31,600 in the first year.

After two years, Sofia's property value increases to approximately $595,000. Her loan balance decreases to

$425,000, creating $170,000 in equity. She refinances the property, accessing $60,000 in cash-out equity while maintaining a manageable loan balance.

Sofia uses this $60,000, along with $40,000 in savings, to purchase a second property valued at $500,000. She puts down 20%, or $100,000, resulting in a loan amount of $400,000. This property generates $3,500 per month in rental income, with a mortgage payment of $2,800, producing $700 in monthly cash flow.

Now Sofia has two properties generating a combined monthly cash flow of $1,500, or $18,000 annually. Both properties continue to appreciate at 4%, adding approximately $44,000 in combined value each year.

After another two years, Sofia repeats the process. She leverages equity and savings to acquire a third property valued at $450,000 with a $90,000 down payment. This property generates $3,200 per month in rental income with a $2,600 payment, producing $600 in monthly cash flow.

At this point, Sofia's portfolio includes three properties with a combined monthly cash flow of $2,100, or $25,200 annually. The total value of her properties is now $1,500,000, and annual appreciation at 4% adds $60,000 in value. Let's analyze Sofia's position after five years. Her portfolio generates over $25,000 in annual cash flow and gains approximately $60,000 in annual appreciation. Combined, this results in over $85,000 in annual financial growth.

Even if Sofia's initial loans carried higher interest rates due to her credit challenges, the overall outcome is highly positive. The combination of income, appreciation, and equity growth far exceeds the additional interest costs.

Sofia also plans her exit strategy. She may choose to sell one property to realize gains, refinance to reduce costs, or hold all properties for long-term income. Each option provides flexibility and opportunity.

This example demonstrates how bank statement mortgage loans can be used as a foundation for long-term wealth building. By leveraging equity, reinvesting profits, and maintaining financial discipline, Sofia transforms her initial approval into a growing portfolio.

It reinforces the final principle of this book: success is not defined by where you start—it is defined by how you grow. With the right strategy, even borrowers with credit challenges can build significant wealth and achieve lasting financial success.

Chapter 13

Advanced Deal Structuring—Combining Bank Statement Loans with Other Strategies

As borrowers and professionals advance beyond the fundamentals of bank statement mortgage loans, a new level of opportunity emerges: combining these loans with other financing strategies to create more powerful, flexible, and scalable deals. Chapter 13 is dedicated to advanced deal structuring—where creativity, knowledge, and strategy intersect to unlock opportunities that go far beyond standard loan approvals. This is where experienced borrowers and investors separate themselves, using multiple tools together to achieve results that would not be possible with a single approach.

At its core, advanced structuring is about integration. Bank statement loans provide a strong foundation by allowing borrowers to qualify based on real income rather than tax returns. However, when combined with other strategies—such as DSCR loans, HELOCs, seller financing, or portfolio lending—the possibilities expand significantly. These combinations allow borrowers to optimize cash flow, leverage equity more efficiently, and scale their investments faster.

One of the most common and effective combinations is the use of bank statement loans alongside DSCR (Debt Service Coverage Ratio) loans. Bank statement loans are ideal for qualifying the borrower based on income, while DSCR loans focus on the property's ability to generate income. By using both strategies together, borrowers can qualify for multiple properties even if their personal income alone would not support additional loans. This creates a dual-qualification system where both the borrower and the property contribute to approval.

Another powerful strategy is the use of home equity lines of credit (HELOCs) in conjunction with bank statement loans. A borrower can use a bank statement loan to acquire a property, allow it to appreciate, and then access the equity through a HELOC. This equity can then be used as a down payment for additional properties, creating a cycle of growth. The key to this strategy is maintaining sufficient equity and managing leverage carefully to avoid overextending.

Seller financing is another advanced tool that can be combined with bank statement loans. In some cases, a seller may be willing to finance a portion of the purchase price, reducing the amount that needs to be financed through a traditional lender.

This can lower the loan-to-value ratio, improve the borrower's profile, and make approval easier. It can also reduce the upfront cash required, allowing borrowers to preserve liquidity for future investments.

Portfolio lending is another avenue for advanced structuring. Some lenders offer portfolio loans that are held in-house rather than sold on the secondary market. These lenders often have more flexibility in their guidelines, allowing for customized solutions that may not fit standard programs. By combining portfolio lending with bank statement loans, borrowers can access unique opportunities and structure deals that align with their specific goals.

Cross-collateralization is another advanced concept that can be used in certain scenarios. This involves using multiple properties as collateral for a single loan or group of loans. While this approach can increase borrowing capacity, it also introduces additional complexity and risk. It should be used carefully and only when the benefits clearly outweigh the potential downsides.

Another important aspect of advanced structuring is optimizing cash flow. This involves analyzing each deal not just for approval, but for long-term profitability. Factors such as interest rates, loan terms, rental income, and operating expenses must all be considered. By structuring deals to maximize cash flow, borrowers can create sustainable income streams that support further growth.

Leverage is a key component of advanced structuring, but it must be managed carefully. While higher leverage can increase returns, it also increases risk. The goal is to find the optimal balance between maximizing opportunity and maintaining stability. This often involves maintaining strong reserves, ensuring positive cash flow, and avoiding excessive debt.

Another critical factor is exit strategy planning. Every advanced deal should include a clear plan for how the borrower will exit or transition the loan. This may involve refinancing into a lower-rate loan, selling the property after appreciation, or holding it for long-term income. Having a defined exit strategy ensures that the deal aligns with the borrower's overall financial goals.

Timing and sequencing also play a major role in advanced structuring. The order in which transactions are executed can impact approval, liquidity, and overall success. For example, acquiring a property with a bank statement loan and then transitioning to a DSCR loan may allow the borrower to free up income capacity for additional purchases. Understanding how to sequence these steps is essential for scaling effectively.

Risk assessment becomes increasingly important at this level. Each additional layer of complexity introduces new variables that must be managed. This includes market risk, interest rate risk, and operational risk. By carefully evaluating each deal and maintaining a disciplined approach, borrowers can mitigate these risks and maintain a stable portfolio.

Another key element is adaptability. Advanced structuring requires the ability to adjust strategies based on changing market conditions, lender guidelines, and personal financial circumstances. Flexibility allows borrowers to take advantage of opportunities and navigate challenges effectively.

Collaboration with experienced professionals is also essential. Advanced deals often involve multiple moving parts, and having the right team—loan officers, financial advisors, and real estate professionals—can make a significant difference. Their expertise can help identify opportunities, structure deals effectively, and avoid potential pitfalls.

Ultimately, advanced deal structuring is about expanding possibilities. It is about moving beyond basic approvals and creating strategies that maximize potential. By combining bank statement loans with other tools, borrowers can unlock new levels of growth and build a more dynamic and resilient portfolio. This chapter reinforces the idea that mastery comes from integration. By understanding how different strategies work together, borrowers can create solutions that go far beyond traditional limitations. As you continue your journey, these advanced techniques will allow you to operate at a higher level and achieve greater success.

Real-Life Math Example: Combining Multiple Strategies for Maximum Growth

Let's explore a comprehensive scenario involving a borrower named Lucas, a self-employed real estate entrepreneur. Lucas has a credit score of 645 and strong bank statement income, but he wants to scale his portfolio quickly using advanced structuring strategies.

Lucas starts by purchasing a property valued at $600,000 using a bank statement loan. He puts down 20%, or $120,000, resulting in a loan amount of $480,000. The property generates $4,000 per month in rental income, with a mortgage payment of $3,200, producing $800 in monthly cash flow.

After one year, the property appreciates by 4%, increasing its value to $624,000. Lucas's loan balance decreases to $470,000, creating $154,000 in equity. He opens a HELOC and accesses $80,000 of this equity.

Lucas uses the $80,000 as a down payment for a second property valued at $400,000, securing a DSCR loan. This property generates $3,200 per month in rental income, with a mortgage payment of $2,600, producing $600 in monthly cash flow.

Now Lucas has two properties generating a combined monthly cash flow of $1,400, or $16,800 annually. Both properties continue to appreciate, adding approximately $40,000 in combined value each year.

Lucas then identifies a third property valued at $500,000 where the seller is willing to finance 10% of the purchase price. Lucas uses $50,000 from savings and $50,000 from the HELOC as his down payment, reducing the amount needed from traditional financing.

The third property generates $3,800 per month in rental income, with a combined payment of $3,000, producing $800 in monthly cash flow. Lucas now has three properties generating $2,200 per month, or $26,400 annually.

Let's analyze Lucas's position. His total property value is now $1,500,000, and annual appreciation at 4% adds $60,000 in value. Combined with his cash flow, Lucas gains over $86,000 annually.

Even with the use of multiple financing strategies, Lucas maintains strong reserves and positive cash flow, ensuring stability. His ability to combine bank statement loans, HELOCs, DSCR loans, and seller financing allows him to scale rapidly while managing risk.

This example demonstrates the power of advanced deal structuring. By integrating multiple strategies, Lucas accelerates his growth and maximizes his opportunities. It reinforces the principle that in bank statement lending, success is not just about approval—it is about innovation and execution.

Chapter 14

Avoiding Common Mistakes and Protecting Your Approval

As borrowers and professionals gain experience with bank statement mortgage loans—especially when working with credit challenges—it becomes increasingly important to understand not only what leads to approval, but also what can derail it. Chapter 14 focuses on the most common mistakes that occur throughout the process and, more importantly, how to avoid them. Even strong borrowers with solid income and assets can face delays or denials if critical details are overlooked. Protecting your approval requires awareness, discipline, and a proactive approach.

One of the most common mistakes is inconsistent or poorly documented bank statement activity. Since bank statement loans rely heavily on deposits to determine income, any irregularities can raise red flags. Large unexplained deposits, inconsistent monthly revenue, or frequent transfers between accounts can create confusion during underwriting. Borrowers often assume that all deposits will be counted as income, but this is not the case. Transfers, one-time deposits, and undocumented funds may be excluded, reducing qualifying income and potentially affecting approval. The solution is to maintain clean, consistent accounts and clearly document any anomalies before submitting the file.

Another frequent issue is misunderstanding the expense factor. Many borrowers assume that their gross deposits will translate directly into qualifying income, only to discover that lenders apply an expense ratio that significantly reduces that amount. Failing to account for this adjustment can lead to unrealistic expectations and unfavorable debt-to-income ratios. To avoid this mistake, borrowers should work with professionals to estimate their qualifying income accurately and explore options such as CPA-prepared profit and loss statements to potentially reduce the expense factor.

Credit behavior during the loan process is another critical area where mistakes often occur. Borrowers may open new accounts, increase credit card balances, or miss payments while their loan is in progress. These actions can negatively impact their credit profile and raise concerns during underwriting. Even a single late payment or significant increase in utilization can trigger additional scrutiny or jeopardize approval. Maintaining strict financial discipline from application to closing is essential.

Another common mistake is insufficient reserves. Borrowers may focus on meeting the minimum down payment requirement without considering the importance of reserves. Lenders view reserves as a key indicator of financial stability, especially for borrowers with credit challenges. A lack of reserves can increase perceived risk and lead to stricter conditions or denial. Building and maintaining adequate reserves—often several months of mortgage payments—can significantly strengthen the file.

Overestimating affordability is another pitfall. Borrowers may qualify for a certain loan amount based on income calculations, but this does not always mean that the loan is financially sustainable. Taking on a mortgage that stretches cash flow too thin can lead to future financial stress and increase the risk of default. It is important to evaluate not just qualification, but comfort and sustainability. A well-structured loan should support long-term stability, not just short-term approval.

Timing mistakes can also impact approval. Applying too early—before credit issues are resolved, income is stabilized, or assets are properly positioned—can lead to unnecessary challenges. Conversely, waiting too long can result in missed opportunities, particularly in appreciating markets. Strategic timing involves balancing readiness with opportunity, ensuring that the borrower's profile is strong while also taking advantage of favorable conditions. Another significant issue is choosing the wrong lender or program. As discussed in previous chapters, lender overlays and guidelines vary widely. Submitting a file to a lender whose requirements do not align with the borrower's profile can result in denial, even if the borrower could qualify elsewhere. Understanding lender preferences and matching the file to the appropriate program is critical for success.

Poor documentation and organization can also create problems. A disorganized file with missing or unclear documents can lead to delays, additional conditions, and frustration. Underwriters rely on clear, complete information to make decisions. Providing well-organized, labeled, and consistent documentation not only speeds up the process but also builds confidence in the file.

Another common mistake is failing to provide clear explanations for credit events. When negative items appear on a credit report without context, underwriters are left to make assumptions. This can increase perceived risk and lead to additional scrutiny. Providing concise, factual explanations supported by documentation helps clarify the situation and demonstrates accountability.

Ignoring the importance of communication is another issue. Delayed responses to conditions, unclear answers, or lack of follow-up can slow down the process and create unnecessary complications. Maintaining open, timely communication with all parties involved ensures that the file progresses smoothly.

Over-leveraging is a more advanced mistake that often occurs when borrowers begin to scale their investments. Taking on too much debt without sufficient reserves or cash flow can increase risk and limit future opportunities. While leverage is a powerful tool, it must be used carefully and strategically to maintain balance and stability.

Another overlooked factor is property selection. Choosing a property that does not align with the borrower's financial profile or lender guidelines can create challenges. This includes properties with limited marketability, inconsistent income potential, or issues identified during appraisal. Selecting the right property is an important part of protecting approval.

Failing to plan for contingencies is another mistake. Unexpected issues can arise during the loan process, from appraisal discrepancies to documentation requests. Having a contingency plan—such as additional reserves or alternative documentation—allows borrowers to respond effectively and keep the process moving forward.

It is also important to avoid relying on assumptions. Each loan is unique, and guidelines can change. What worked for one borrower may not apply to another. Verifying information, confirming requirements, and staying informed are essential for avoiding surprises. Ultimately, protecting your approval is about attention to detail and proactive management. By identifying potential issues early and addressing them before they become problems, borrowers can significantly improve their chances of success.

This chapter reinforces the idea that success in bank statement mortgage lending is not just about strategy—it is about execution. Avoiding mistakes is just as important as applying the right techniques. By maintaining discipline, staying organized, and approaching the process with a proactive mindset, borrowers can navigate challenges and achieve consistent approvals.

Real-Life Math Example: Avoiding Mistakes to Protect Approval

Let's consider a detailed scenario involving a borrower named Kevin, a self-employed contractor with strong income but a credit score of 635. Kevin is purchasing a home valued at $540,000 and plans to put down 20%, or $108,000, resulting in a loan amount of $432,000.

Over the past 12 months, Kevin has deposited $300,000 into his bank account, averaging $25,000 per month. The lender applies an expense factor of 50%, resulting in a qualifying monthly income of $12,500. Kevin's monthly debts total $3,000, and the estimated mortgage payment is $3,200. This brings his total monthly obligations to $6,200. Dividing $6,200 by $12,500 results in a debt-to-income ratio of approximately 50%, which is acceptable but near the upper limit.

During the underwriting process, Kevin makes a critical mistake. He deposits $20,000 into his account from a personal loan without documenting the source. The underwriter flags this deposit and excludes it from income calculations, raising concerns about his financial stability.

Additionally, Kevin increases his credit card balances by $5,000, raising his monthly obligations by $200. This increases his total monthly debt to $6,400. Recalculating his DTI, we divide $6,400 by $12,500, resulting in approximately 51%, pushing him beyond acceptable guidelines.

At this point, Kevin's approval is at risk. However, he takes corrective action. He provides documentation showing that the $20,000 deposit was a one-time loan and not part of his income. He also pays down his credit card balances, reducing his monthly obligations back to $6,200.

Now let's recalculate his DTI. Dividing $6,200 by $12,500 returns to approximately 50%, bringing him back within acceptable limits. Kevin also increases his reserves by adding $10,000 in savings, bringing his total reserves to $50,000. This covers approximately 15 months of mortgage payments, strengthening his profile.

Let's analyze the impact of avoiding these mistakes. Without correction, Kevin's increased DTI and undocumented deposit could have led to denial. By addressing these issues, he restores his eligibility and strengthens his file.

From a financial perspective, Kevin's monthly cash flow remains stable. With income of $12,500 and obligations of $6,200, he has $6,300 in remaining cash flow each month. Over a year, this equals $75,600 in excess cash flow.

Additionally, his property is expected to appreciate at 4%, adding $21,600 in value during the first year. Combined with his cash flow, this creates a strong financial position.

Kevin's experience highlights the importance of discipline and awareness during the loan process. By avoiding common mistakes and taking corrective action when necessary, he is able to protect his approval and achieve his goal.

This example reinforces the principle that small missteps can have significant consequences, but they can also be corrected with the right approach. Protecting approval is not just about meeting guidelines—it is about maintaining control throughout the process.

Chapter 15

The Ultimate Blueprint—From Credit Challenges to Financial Freedom

As we arrive at the final chapter of this book, everything comes together into one complete, actionable blueprint. This is where knowledge turns into transformation. Throughout this series, you have learned how to navigate bank statement mortgage loans, overcome credit challenges, structure strong files, leverage compensating factors, choose the right lenders, and build long-term strategies. Chapter 15 is about consolidating all of these principles into a repeatable system that not only gets loans approved but also builds lasting financial freedom.

The first step in this blueprint is clarity. Financial freedom is not a vague concept—it is a defined outcome. For some, it means owning a home. For others, it means building a portfolio of income-producing properties. For many, it means creating enough passive income to cover living expenses and achieve independence. Defining your goal is critical because it determines the strategy you will use. Without clarity, even the best tools and knowledge can lead to scattered results.

Once the goal is defined, the next step is building a foundation. This foundation consists of your financial profile: income, assets, credit, and cash flow. Even with credit challenges, this foundation can be strengthened. Consistent bank statement deposits, organized financial records, and disciplined money management create stability. This stability becomes the starting point for every opportunity that follows.

The third step is strategic positioning. This is where everything you have learned about structuring files, managing debt, and optimizing income comes into play. Positioning is about presenting your financial profile in the strongest possible way. It is about aligning your strengths with lender expectations and minimizing perceived risk. This step transforms your foundation into an approvable profile.

The fourth step is execution. This includes selecting the right lender, submitting a well-structured file, and navigating underwriting with precision. Execution requires attention to detail, responsiveness, and discipline. It is where preparation meets action. A strong execution phase ensures that the work done in earlier steps translates into a successful approval.

The fifth step is acquisition. This is where the loan becomes a tangible asset—a property that can generate income, appreciate in value, and serve as a foundation for future growth. Acquisition is not the end goal; it is the beginning of the wealth-building process. The sixth step is optimization.

After acquiring a property, the focus shifts to maximizing its performance. This includes increasing rental income, reducing expenses, and improving cash flow. Optimization also involves monitoring market conditions and identifying opportunities for refinancing or repositioning the asset.

The seventh step is scaling. As discussed in previous chapters, scaling involves using the success of one transaction to fuel the next. This may include leveraging equity, reinvesting profits, or combining multiple financing strategies. Scaling transforms individual transactions into a growing portfolio.

The eighth step is protection. As your portfolio grows, so does your responsibility to manage risk. This includes maintaining reserves, avoiding over-leverage, and ensuring that each property contributes positively to your overall financial position. Protection ensures that growth is sustainable and resilient.

The ninth step is transition. Over time, as your credit improves and your financial profile strengthens, you can transition from higher-cost bank statement loans to lower-cost traditional financing. This reduces expenses, increases cash flow, and enhances long-term profitability. Transitioning is a key component of optimizing your financial position. The final step is freedom. Financial freedom is achieved when your income—whether from properties, investments, or business activities—covers your expenses and provides flexibility. At this stage, your financial system works for you, rather than the other way around. This is the ultimate goal of the blueprint.

One of the most important aspects of this blueprint is that it is adaptable. Every borrower's journey is different, and the steps may be applied in different ways depending on individual circumstances. The key is to understand the principles and apply them consistently.

Another critical element is discipline. Success in this system requires consistent effort, thoughtful decision-making, and the ability to stay focused on long-term goals. There will be challenges along the way, but each challenge is an opportunity to refine your strategy and strengthen your approach.

It is also important to recognize the role of patience. Wealth building is a process, not an event. While bank statement mortgage loans provide access to opportunities, the true benefits are realized over time. Appreciation, equity growth, and cash flow all compound, creating exponential results.

Education remains a cornerstone of success. The more you understand about lending, real estate, and financial strategy, the more effectively you can navigate the system. Continuous learning allows you to adapt to changes and stay ahead of opportunities.

Collaboration is another key factor. Working with experienced professionals—loan officers, real estate agents, financial advisors—can provide valuable insights and support. A strong team enhances your ability to execute the blueprint effectively.

Ultimately, this chapter is about empowerment. It is about recognizing that credit challenges are not limitations—they are starting points. With the right strategies and mindset, they can be overcome, and they can even become advantages by pushing you to learn and grow.

The blueprint outlined in this chapter is not theoretical. It is practical, actionable, and proven. It has been applied by countless borrowers and professionals to achieve real results. By following these steps, you can move from uncertainty to clarity, from challenges to opportunities, and from approval to financial freedom.

As you close this book, remember that the journey is yours to create. The knowledge is now in your hands. The strategies are available to you. The only question that remains is how you will apply them.

Your financial future is not determined by your past—it is

shaped by your actions today.

Real-Life Math Example: From First Loan to Financial Freedom

Let's conclude with a comprehensive scenario that brings the entire blueprint to life. Meet Andrea, a self-employed consultant with a credit score of 640 who begins her journey with a bank statement mortgage loan.

Andrea purchases her first property for $500,000, putting down 20%, or $100,000. Her loan amount is $400,000, and her monthly mortgage payment is $2,800. The property generates $3,600 per month in rental income, resulting in $800 in monthly cash flow.

In the first year, Andrea earns $9,600 in net income and benefits from 4% appreciation, adding $20,000 in value. Her total gain for the year is $29,600.

After two years, her property value increases to approximately $540,000, and her loan balance decreases to $385,000, creating $155,000 in equity. She refinances and accesses $60,000 in cash-out funds.

Andrea uses this $60,000, along with $40,000 in savings, to purchase a second property valued at $500,000. This property generates $3,500 per month in rental income with a $2,800 payment, producing $700 in monthly cash flow.

Now Andrea has two properties generating $1,500 per month, or $18,000 annually. Both properties appreciate, adding approximately $40,000 in combined value each year.

After another two years, Andrea repeats the process, acquiring a third property valued at $450,000 with a $90,000 down payment. This property generates $3,200 per month in rental income with a $2,600 payment, producing $600 in monthly cash flow.

At this stage, Andrea's portfolio generates $2,100 per month, or $25,200 annually, and her properties appreciate by approximately $60,000 per year.

Andrea then transitions her loans to lower interest rates as her credit improves, reducing her monthly payments by $300 per property. This increases her total cash flow by $900 per month, bringing it to $3,000 per month, or $36,000 annually.

Over time, Andrea continues to scale, reinvest profits, and optimize her portfolio. After ten years, she owns multiple properties generating over $8,000 per month in cash flow, or $96,000 annually, while her portfolio value exceeds $3 million.

Let's summarize her journey. Starting with a single property, Andrea builds a portfolio that generates substantial income and equity. Even with initial credit challenges and higher interest rates, her long-term strategy allows her to achieve financial independence.

This example demonstrates the full power of the blueprint. By combining strategic planning, disciplined execution, and long-term vision, Andrea transforms her financial future.

It reinforces the final and most important principle of this book: financial freedom is not reserved for those with perfect credit—it is available to those with the right strategy and the determination to follow it.

Final Thoughts

As you reach the end of this book, it is important to pause and reflect on how far you have come—not just in terms of information, but in terms of perspective. What once may have felt like a complex, confusing, or even impossible system should now feel structured, understandable, and most importantly, actionable. The world of bank statement mortgage loans, especially for borrowers with credit challenges, is not a mystery reserved for a select few. It is a system—one that rewards knowledge, preparation, and strategy. And now, you are equipped with all three.

One of the most powerful realizations from this journey is that credit challenges are not permanent barriers. They are temporary conditions within a much larger financial picture. Traditional lending systems often reduce borrowers to a single number, but as you have learned, that number does not define your true financial capability. Your income, your discipline, your consistency, and your ability to adapt all matter—and in the bank statement mortgage loan space, they matter a great deal. This shift in perspective alone can change the way you approach your financial future.

Throughout this book, a consistent theme has emerged: control. While you cannot change the past, you can control how your present is structured and how your future is planned. You can control your income patterns, your savings habits, your debt management, and the way your financial story is presented. This level of control is empowering. It allows you to move from a reactive mindset—waiting to see if you qualify—to a proactive one, where you build a profile that is designed to succeed.

Another key takeaway is the importance of strategy. Approval is not about luck or timing alone; it is about alignment. It is about aligning your financial profile with the right lender, the right program, and the right structure. It is about understanding how each component—income, credit, assets, and documentation—works together to create a complete picture. When these elements are aligned, approval becomes not just possible, but predictable.

It is also important to recognize that this process is not a one-time event. The strategies you have learned are not limited to a single loan or transaction. They are tools that can be used repeatedly, refined over time, and scaled into larger opportunities. Whether your goal is to purchase a home, build a portfolio of investment properties, or create long-term financial independence, the principles remain the same. Each success builds upon the last, creating momentum that carries you forward. Patience plays a critical role in this journey.

While the strategies outlined in this book can accelerate your progress, true financial growth takes time. Equity builds gradually. Cash flow increases over time. Credit improves with consistent behavior. The key is to remain focused and committed, even when results are not immediate. Every step you take—every payment made on time, every dollar saved, every strategic decision—contributes to your long-term success.

Discipline is equally important. The ability to maintain consistency in your financial behavior is what transforms short-term wins into lasting results. This includes managing your credit responsibly, maintaining strong reserves, and avoiding unnecessary risks. Discipline ensures that the progress you make is not only achieved but sustained.

It is also worth emphasizing the importance of learning from challenges. Not every loan will be approved on the first attempt. Not every deal will go exactly as planned. But each experience provides valuable insight. A denial is not a failure—it is feedback. It reveals areas that can be improved and strategies that can be adjusted. By approaching challenges with a mindset of growth, you turn obstacles into opportunities.

Another critical element is adaptability. The financial landscape is constantly changing. Lender guidelines evolve, market conditions shift, and new opportunities emerge. The ability to adapt—to adjust your strategy, explore new options, and respond to changes—is essential for long-term success. Flexibility allows you to stay ahead of challenges and take advantage of opportunities as they arise.

As you move forward, it is important to remember that you do not have to navigate this journey alone. Building a strong network of professionals—loan officers, real estate agents, financial advisors—can provide valuable support and guidance. These individuals bring experience, insight, and perspective that can enhance your decision-making and streamline your process.

At the same time, your role remains central. No one understands your goals, your circumstances, or your vision better than you do. The knowledge you have gained from this book empowers you to take an active role in your financial journey. It allows you to ask the right questions, make informed decisions, and take ownership of your outcomes.

One of the most inspiring aspects of this journey is the realization that financial freedom is not reserved for a select group of people. It is accessible to anyone willing to learn, plan, and act. It does not require perfect credit, unlimited resources, or ideal circumstances. It requires understanding, effort, and persistence. The strategies in this book are designed to bridge the gap between where you are and where you want to be.

As you apply these strategies, you will begin to see changes—not just in your financial situation, but in your confidence and mindset. Each step forward reinforces your ability to succeed. Each success builds your belief in what is possible. Over time, these small steps compound into significant progress, creating a trajectory that leads to long-term growth and stability.

It is also important to keep your long-term vision in focus. Short-term decisions should always align with your broader goals. Whether you are building a portfolio, increasing your income, or creating a legacy for your family, every action should contribute to that vision. This alignment ensures that your efforts are not just productive, but purposeful.

As this book comes to a close, the most important message is this: your financial future is in your hands. The tools, strategies, and knowledge you need are now available to you. What matters most is how you use them. The path forward may not always be easy, but it is clear. With consistency, discipline, and strategic thinking, you can navigate challenges, seize opportunities, and create the financial life you envision.

The journey does not end here—it begins here.

How to Get a Personalized Bank Statement Mortgage Review

If you found this book helpful, you may want to see how these strategies apply to your specific financial situation.

Bank statement mortgage lending is highly customized—your deposits, income patterns, expense ratios, credit profile, property type, and long-term goals all play a role in determining what you qualify for and how your loan should be structured.

Every borrower's situation is different. The way your income flows through your accounts, how your business operates, your credit history, the property you are purchasing or refinancing, and current lender guidelines all impact your options. The strategies and examples in this book are designed to teach you how bank statement mortgage loans work—but your actual qualifying income, loan amount, and loan structure can only be determined by analyzing your real financial profile.

If you would like a no-obligation Bank Statement Mortgage review, you can request one here:

Email: info@FinibiMortgage.com

A licensed mortgage broker will review your bank statements, income structure, credit profile, and goals, and explain what bank statement mortgage options may be available to you—including:

• 12-month and 24-month bank statement programs• Personal vs business bank statement qualification• Primary residence and investment property financing• Cash-out refinance and equity access strategies• Advanced structuring to maximize qualifying income

No cost. No pressure. No obligation.

Sincerely,

Joseph G. Correa

Finibi Mortgage Inc.

Licensed Mortgage Broker

About the Author

Joseph G. Correa is a licensed mortgage broker and the founder of Finibi Mortgage, a Florida-based brokerage specializing in bank statement mortgage loans, non-QM lending, and strategic real estate financing solutions for self-employed borrowers, entrepreneurs, and investors.

With more than two decades of experience in mortgage lending, underwriting, and deal structuring, Joseph has helped thousands of clients qualify for real estate using alternative income documentation, unlocking opportunities that traditional lending often restricts.

Unlike traditional loan officers who rely strictly on tax returns and W-2 income, Joseph's approach focuses on real cash flow, income structuring, and financial strategy. He believes that borrowers should not be limited by how income is reported on paper, but instead empowered by how income is actually earned and managed.

Joseph is widely recognized for his expertise in:

• Bank statement mortgage loans• Self-employed borrower financing• Non-QM and alternative income lending• Investment property and portfolio financing• Cash-out refinance and equity strategies• Advanced mortgage loan structuring

Through his education platform, Finibi Academy, Joseph has trained tens of thousands of students worldwide in mortgage strategy, real estate investing, credit optimization, and financial independence.

He created the **Bank Statement Mortgage Loan Mastery Series** to provide a clear, step-by-step roadmap for borrowers and professionals who want to qualify for real estate without relying on traditional income documentation.

His mission is simple: To help people use their real income—not just their tax returns—to qualify, invest, and build long-term wealth.

When he is not structuring loans or writing, Joseph works with clients across the United States to design customized mortgage strategies that align with their financial goals, income structure, and long-term investment plans.

The Bank Statement Mortgage Loan Mastery Series Roadmap

The Complete Guide to Qualifying for Real Estate Using Bank Statements Instead of Tax Returns

The purpose of the **Bank Statement Mortgage Loan Mastery Series** is to give borrowers, investors, and mortgage professionals the exact strategies used by lenders and underwriters—translated into simple, practical steps you can apply in real life.

This series takes you from beginner to advanced mastery of how to qualify, structure, and scale real estate financing using bank statements instead of traditional income.

Each book builds on the last. You are not just learning how to get approved—you are learning how to control your approvals.

Book 1 — Bank Statement Mortgage Loan Fundamentals

Learn how bank statement loans work, how income is calculated, and why tax returns are no longer required for many borrowers.

Book 2 — Personal Bank Statement Mortgage Loans

Learn how to qualify using personal accounts, structure

deposits, and maximize usable income.

Book 3 — Business Bank Statement Mortgage Loans

Understand how lenders analyze business revenue, apply expense ratios, and use P&Ls.

Book 4 — Bank Statement Loans for Self-Employed Borrowers

Master how entrepreneurs qualify and structure income for approval.

Book 5 — Bank Statement Loans for Primary Residences

Learn how to buy or refinance your home using bank statement income.

Book 6 — Bank Statement Loans for Investment Properties

Discover how to scale rental portfolios using bank statement + DSCR strategies.

Book 7 — Jumbo Bank Statement Mortgage Loans

Learn how to finance high-value properties with advanced requirements and structuring.

Book 8 — Bank Statement Loan Refinancing & Cash-Out Strategies

Unlock equity, reduce payments, and reinvest capital using bank statement refinancing.

Book 9 — Bank Statement Loans with Credit Challenges

Learn how to qualify even with lower credit using compensating factors and strategy.

Book 10 — Advanced Bank Statement Mortgage Loan Structuring

Engineer approvals using deposits, expense ratios, and lender guidelines.

This series is designed to move you from understanding → execution → mastery.

By the end, you will not just know how to qualify—you will know how to structure deals like a professional.

Educational & Financial Disclaimer

The **Bank Statement Mortgage Loan Mastery Series** is intended for educational and informational purposes only.

This content is designed to help readers understand bank statement mortgage lending, real estate financing strategies, and income structuring concepts. It is not financial, legal, tax, or investment advice.

Joseph G. Correa and Live Stronger Faster are not acting as your personal financial advisor, attorney, accountant, or mortgage professional through this publication.

Mortgage guidelines, underwriting standards, interest rates, and loan programs vary by lender and may change at any time without notice.

All examples in this series are for illustration purposes only and do not guarantee approval or results.

Always consult with licensed professionals before making financial decisions.

Risk Disclosure

Bank statement mortgage lending and real estate investing involve risk.

Income fluctuations, interest rate changes, market conditions, and lender guidelines can all impact loan approval and financial outcomes.

Borrowing against real estate or using leverage increases both potential returns and risks.

Failure to repay a loan may result in foreclosure and loss of property.

Cash flow, rental income, and appreciation are not guaranteed.

All strategies in this series are educational and must be evaluated based on your individual financial situation.

You are solely responsible for your financial decisions.

www.ingramcontent.com/pod-product-compliance
Ingram Content Group UK Ltd.
Pitfield, Milton Keynes, MK11 3LW, UK
UKHW020159290926
15471UKWH00005B/956